Praise for *Scale with Purpose*

"Supported by a wealth of real-world examples, *Scale with Purpose* will teach you not only the correct practices, but also the guiding principles that will help you build a business that matters."

TIM WILLIAMS, author of *Positioning for Professionals*

"Thoroughly researched, highly practical, and refreshingly honest, *Scale with Purpose* is an indispensable guide for service entrepreneurs who want to grow beyond survival and intentionally design profitable, sustainable firms."

MARY DELANEY, CEO of Karbon

"*Scale with Purpose* is packed with practical wisdom, clarity, and frameworks that move you from the chaos of growth to the calm of intentional scale."

PAUL DUNN, founder of B1G1 and Results Corporation

"*Scale with Purpose* teaches how growth should be a choice you accept carefully when the marketplace sends you those signals, ensuring that your firm still works for you and not the other way around."

DAVID C. BAKER, author of *The Business of Expertise*

"Highly researched, with real examples, this book is a solid blend of Jason M. Blumer and Ian Vacin's deep expertise and genuine empathy for business leaders, which makes it both heavy duty and very readable."

KAREN REYBURN, author of *The Accountant Marketer* and founder of The Profitable Firm

"*Scale with Purpose* shows leaders how to communicate better, lead smarter, and grow intentionally. Don't scale by accident. Lead on purpose."

L. GARY BOOMER, founder of Boomer Consulting

"*Scale with Purpose* is a roadmap that turns talent, technology, and transformation into a grand slam and shows exactly how to blast through the scaling plateaus that stall most firms."

ALLAN KOLTIN, founder and CEO of Koltin Consulting Group

"Jason M. Blumer and Ian Vacin's deep understanding of the intersection between people, processes, and technology makes this essential reading for any leader serious about scaling with intention."

PROMISE PHELON, founder of Growth Warrior Capital and former Silicon Valley tech CEO

"*Scale with Purpose* provides thoughtful and grounded guidance for service entrepreneurs scaling their firms, with practical insights on leadership, capacity, and organizational growth."

ILAN ADLER, Chancellor's professor in industrial engineering and operations research at the University of California, Berkeley

"Jason M. Blumer played a huge role in helping me start my first business; it would not have happened without him. This book is a trustworthy roadmap for anyone serious about intentional growth."

DAN MALL, founder of SuperFriendly and author of *Design That Scales*

"Growing a service business poses unique challenges. This book shares real-world frameworks to help leaders operate and scale a people-powered business."

STEVEN ALDRICH, entrepreneur, board member, and investor

"Jason M. Blumer and Ian Vacin distill years of deep industry experience into practical strategies that actually work. *Scale with Purpose* will change how you think about your firm and your future."

CARLA CALDWELL, founder of Candella Accounting and Advisory Services

"Here for the first time for service entrepreneurs is a practical guide on how to scale to your success. Using data from over 100 interviews, Jason M. Blumer and Ian Vacin codify success frameworks specific to professional service firms."

JIM MCGINNIS, CEO of Vanco and former CEO of MyCase

"If you're serious about leading your team beyond 8, 20, or even 50 people, *Scale with Purpose* shows you how to do it with clarity and confidence."

BRANDON HALL, founder of Hall CPA

"At a time when accounting firms face a choice—stagnate or reinvent—*Scale with Purpose* offers the clearest path forward. This book isn't just advice; it's a deeply-researched, field-tested blueprint!"

DAVE YUAN, founder of Tidemark and former general partner of TCV

"*Scale with Purpose* provides actionable frameworks and roadmaps for navigating the unique challenges that arise from a leadership, financial, and organizational perspective as companies grow."

GEETA ARORA, former general manager of Swag.com

"*Scale with Purpose* provides a compelling roadmap for the ongoing reinvention required to scale a services business. Rather than relying solely on broad frameworks, it dives deep into the real-world complexities and nuances of how these strategies unfold in practice."

TYSON CHAPMAN, COO of Platform Accounting Group

"With clarity, authenticity, and precision, this book empowers service-based leaders to scale with intention, avoid common pitfalls, and build truly sustainable success."

JAY VICTOR, senior director at Microsoft and former director at the Walt Disney Company

"After years of helping agency leaders grow, I've seen that the struggles Jason M. Blumer and Ian Vacin describe are universal to service firms. *Scale with Purpose* distills challenges into practical frameworks that give leaders the clarity, confidence, and courage to scale with intention."

KARL SAKAS, executive coach and founder of Sakas & Company

"Successful entrepreneurs eventually grow their business to the size where things start to break. Typically, revenue outpaces organizational structure and health. Jason M. Blumer and Ian Vacin unpack a brilliant methodology of how service businesses can work through this messy middle."

KADE WILCOX, serial entrepreneur and founder of Boost Patients and FlatlandWorks

"The pervasive belief is that the growth of professional services businesses is solely a factor of one mathematical formula: billed hours per billable resource. Jason M. Blumer and Ian Vacin bring to life a better reality. Identify your exclusives. Perfect that. Do less. Make more money. Scale (grow)."

G. T. "TOBY" STANSELL, executive chair at NxTrek

SCALE WITH PURPOSE

SCALE

with

PURPOSE

The Service Entrepreneur's Guide to *Intentional Growth*

JASON M. BLUMER & **IAN VACIN**

PAGE TWO

Cataloguing in publication information is
available from Library and Archives Canada.
ISBN 978-1-77458-563-4 (paperback)
ISBN 978-1-77458-570-2 (ebook)

Page Two
pagetwo.com

Page Two™ is a trademark owned by
Page Two Strategies Inc., and is used under
license by authorized licensees

Cover, interior design, and
illustrations by Cameron McKague

scalewithpurpose.info

*This book is dedicated to all the service entrepreneurs,
who are the foundation on which our economies move and grow.
We salute you! This book is also dedicated to those who
keep these service entrepreneurs in check—the operational and
integrational unsung heroes that also move their service
organizations forward. Julie Shipp was that for Jason,
and Andi Ancheta was that for Ian. They are part of our success
(and were often the very reason for success). We also want to
thank our families, who bear the weight of the dedication
it takes to put a book like this out into the world. Thank you!*

Contents

Introduction

---

*When we were smaller, I knew what everyone was working
on. It was manageable because of the size of the team and
the number of clients. Now we're approaching 15 employees, and
my biggest struggle right now is that everything I thought
I knew, I don't know anymore. I don't have my finger on the pulse
with (a) what everyone's working on, (b) how our clients are
being serviced, and (c) how much time things are taking. My biggest
fear is if one of my amazing team members who has been with
me from the start leaves and we can't execute on our promises.*

JENNIFER GREEN
(FOUNDER AND PARTNER OF JADE CONSULTING;
15 EMPLOYEES)

The Struggles of Growth

Ian Vacin

Founded over twenty-five years ago near Toronto, Canada, Jade
Consulting was one of the first accounting firms in North America
to move fully into the cloud in 2013—in an industry not known
for tech savviness or risk taking. I know Jennifer Green and her
team personally from a roundtable discussion I led back in those
days, and I have watched them build an amazing business over the
last decade, tripling it in the past three years alone since bringing

1

on business partner Michelle Felip. These ladies are smart, savvy, and client obsessed and brilliant business operators. So when I interviewed Jennifer to discuss the research for this book, I was surprised to hear her say, "Everything I thought I knew, I don't know anymore." If anyone could grow their business quickly from 1 to 5 to 10 to 20 employees, Jennifer would be that person. So why did she feel this way? It just didn't make sense to me.

Jennifer's quote isn't a reflection of her business or who she is as an entrepreneurial owner of her firm. It reflects where she is in the evolution of her business. As you might know, running a service organization based on knowledge work is hard. You probably run one yourself. And, as you know, it gets much more difficult the larger the organization becomes.

Jennifer's statement is a reflection of what most entrepreneurs of service organizations say to themselves at some point as they grow their organization from 1 to 20 employees. The voices in their heads (and maybe your head) might say something like this:

- Why are client issues happening, and why am I not aware of them sooner?

- Why is our profit margin on our services dropping when it has been steadily increasing over the past few years?

- Why does it seem like our team is getting lazier and less productive?

- Why don't I have enough time to work with clients directly like I want to?

- Why do I feel like my staff is unhappy and looking to leave?

- What happens if my best employee does leave? What will I do?

- Why is this all happening right now? We've never experienced these problems before.

- What am I actually doing? Why am I not enjoying this anymore?

- Maybe I'm just not good enough or the right person for this?

If you think and feel any of these things, you are not alone. While writing this book, we—Jason Blumer and Ian Vacin—spent time interviewing over a hundred high-performing entrepreneurial owners from various service organizations and industries, including accounting, legal, consulting, and marketing. We wanted to validate what we had heard and observed in our thirty-plus years each talking, listening, advising, consulting, and mentoring the owners of knowledge-based service organizations. Jennifer's sentiment wasn't new; it was something we have heard throughout the years. In our interviews with these owners, we found that more than 95 percent experienced what Jennifer had when growing their firms.

So what was different with the 5 percent of firm owners who did not feel this way? What did they do differently, and why?

Blazing Through the First Scaling Plateau

Before growing, we focused on improving profit margin rather than increasing top-line revenue and employee count. Our focus was on getting our operations running more efficiently first. Once we had that, we focused on smart growth. By clearly understanding our future demand, we were able to back into the numbers of how many people (and in what roles) we needed to support the revenue and revenue growth.

MARY INMAN AND JESSICA HENNESSEY
(CFO AND CEO, RESPECTIVELY, OF 3 MEDIA WEB; 23 EMPLOYEES)

I want to introduce you to Jessica Hennessey and Mary Inman of 3 Media Web—a web design and digital marketing agency producing $4 million in annual revenue and serving over 150 clients. 3 Media Web was founded in 2001; Jessica and Mary bought the firm in 2023 from the prior owner, Marc Avila (now a strategic advisor). Since starting at the firm in 2019, they have helped grow the company from 9 to 23 employees and from $2 million to $4 million in annual revenue, and they aspire to achieve their global maximum in enterprise value by growing to almost 50 employees while generating well over $6 million in annual revenue.

But it gets more interesting. Jess and Mary didn't join as executives; they started in 2019 as the digital marketing director and sales director, respectively. At that time, profit had plateaued, and Marc, like many founders, probably had the same questions that Jennifer had swirling in her head. As Mary said:

> Marc was an amazing developer and super smart. He built a solid business by focusing on exceptional client work. But like many founders, he wasn't formally trained in business management. His mindset was if the bills were paid, things were good. What he needed was a strategic partner, someone who could zoom out, analyze the revenue streams, understand our ideal clients, refine pricing, and build scalability into the model.

And as Mary and Jess got further into the business, they started digging into the financial and operational details. With some quick back-of-the-napkin calculations, they realized that the company wasn't profitable on its core service, websites. What initially looked like a sales issue turned out to be a business model issue. Around that time, they were reading books like *Traction* by Gino Wickman, and they began pulling together the leadership team, including Sara Spector-Brown, who was leading operations, to figure out what to do next. Jess recounted the pivotal conversation:

> At the meeting, Marc said, "I love selling but don't love running the business." And I said, "I like doing digital marketing, but I would rather run the business." And Sara said, "I hate spreadsheets, but I love HR." And Mary said, "I have an accounting degree, and I love numbers." That moment of openness from Marc, his willingness to let go and trust the team, was a turning point. We all shifted roles, and from that point forward, we began to see real traction and real profit.

Once the organizational structure and strategic direction were set, the leadership team asked themselves, "Do we have the right people sitting in the right seats doing the right kind of work? We need to project out how our structure would change over two, three, and even five years from now."

In the process of growing from 9 to 15 to 23 employees, they moved contractors into full-time roles, they reworked who did what across the organization, they formed service-delivery pods around their service lines, and they added firm scaffolding to help manage the collective operations. They did all of this while avoiding the struggles that almost everyone faces when tackling the first scaling plateau that occurs, per our research, on average at 10 employees and exists between 8 and 20 employees.

SCALING PLATEAU

A scaling plateau is a point in time when there is a significant slowdown in the growth of a business or it has become non-responsive to normal cyclical growth tactics. Often called a growth ceiling, this is when the organization has usually maximized its potential within its current operational structure, its current team design, its market foci, or the wily leadership skills needed to break the ceiling. This can truly be frustrating and hard on entrepreneurial leaders, as they don't often know how to surmount the scaling plateau.

It was stories like this that motivated the two of us to come together to write this book. We have both been blessed to work with thousands of entrepreneurs leading service organizations around the globe through our collective work coaching our clients and teams and leading our businesses as founders. We also bring our individual expertise to the partnership: Jason's experience in consulting in his businesses Blumer CPAs and Thriveal, which focus on high-level advisory and consulting for service businesses and entrepreneurs, and Ian's experience building technology solutions that focus on the intricacies of rapidly scaling strategic management systems, through his leadership and management in companies like Intuit, Xero, and his own business, Karbon. Like you, we have not been immune to the scaling plateaus that Jennifer Green so eloquently articulated. Our paths haven't been all rainbows and unicorns. Jason went through his own ups and downs along with his partner, Julie Shipp, to finally embrace what it means to lead two full-time service-based growing entrepreneurial businesses. I pivoted hard into one market and then back again in my global software business supporting the growth and capacity knowledge work of service entrepreneurs all over the world. Both of us have leaned on partners and community, experienced ups and downs, honed practices, and learned continually to figure out the principles and tools found in this book. As a result, this book is a culmination of so many minds, so many influences, and the many lessons other entrepreneurs have taught us along the way.

You'll hear some more of our stories as we dive deep into our own experiences, failures, successes, and lessons learned as we go through the book. We'll be telling our own stories in our own voices—look for the headings that say "Ian Vacin" and "Jason Blumer" to tell you who's talking in each chapter and occasionally when the other one takes over mid-chapter. Our purpose is to give you—the entrepreneurial owner of a service organization with up to 50 employees—a roadmap to navigate and accelerate through these scaling plateaus, like Mary and Jess from 3 Media Web did. Maybe you are just starting your business and wondering what it takes to achieve your definition of success. Maybe you are around 6 to 8 employees in size and looking to avoid the dangers that other firm owners have mentioned are lurking around the corner as you continue to push forward in terms of growth. Perhaps you are like Jennifer Green and currently in the weeds of a scaling plateau looking for answers. Or maybe you have already successfully navigated the first scaling plateau and are looking to put a roadmap in place to accelerate through the next one. Whatever situation you find yourself in, the stories we'll tell, the theories we'll explain, and the solutions we'll outline in this book will help you in your quest for the maximum enterprise value of your firm. Our dream is to help you reach your dream.

However, we didn't want to water things down when we wrote the book. Like running a firm, this isn't going to be easy. There are no silver bullets, no checklist of simple takeaways, and no one to hold your hand and tell you what to do. There is a lot to running a service organization, and the changes required to move from 8 to 20 employees aren't easy. But they are necessary, and you can certainly do them. You wouldn't have picked this book up unless you wanted the answers. And rest assured, this book has the answers.

Speaking of the Facts

When we say we have the answers, we aren't saying it to be arrogant or claim we have *all* the answers. No one does. When we discussed writing this book, both of us had our own version of what the answer was to scaling a firm and getting through various scaling plateaus. Shockingly, after working through our versions, we found the core fundamentals of what we each believed were very similar. That came again from our lucky positions sitting on the ground floor with access, visibility, and insight into thousands of firms just like yours. However, we didn't want to rest on our prior experiences and insights alone.

We treated our understanding and answer to the scaling plateau problem as a hypothesis—one we needed to test before we had the right to be able to write. Unlike other books in the service-organization business nonfiction category, we wanted to be confident that our advice and roadmap were based on fact—not instinct, hearsay, or intuition. We set out to complete and use three research vehicles to validate our hypotheses and solidify our findings prior to writing the book:

Qualitative one-on-one interviews. Over the course of a year, we interviewed over a hundred entrepreneurial leaders of service organizations for up to an hour each. They came from a variety of service sectors, but mostly from the accounting, consulting, and marketing agency industries. Ian is a trained researcher, so we had proper screening, research guides, and moderation. You'll see some of that research come to life in the stories you'll read about throughout the book. If you want more information, you can visit the book's website, scalewithpurpose.info.

Ongoing long-term cross-sectional study. Luckily, at Ian's company (Karbon), he has been running a long-term industry-specific quantitative study that follows accounting firm performance. Started in late 2017, the Karbon Practice Excellence study has been continuously running, even through the time of writing. Over seven years, more than 2,500 firms have completed this thirty-minute survey, which measures a firm's strengths and opportunities across its business functions and compares the results to those of similar firms across the globe. The assessment's purpose is to inform firm owners on how to be effective business owners and entrepreneurs. Accounting firms aren't necessarily legal or design agencies, but the research study focuses on the business side of organizations, rather than the technical side, which makes it relevant to all service organizations. As we go through the book, you will see facts, figures, and references to this wealth of information to benchmark and explain the effectiveness of various approaches. If you want more information on the study, go to karbonhq.com/practice-excellence.

Focused quantitative research. Our third research vehicle was inspired by the book's content itself. From the hypotheses that we had, we designed a dedicated quantitative survey to validate and substantiate the various topics and points we make throughout the book. This twelve-minute survey was conducted throughout 2025 in conjunction with the writing and publishing of the book. As with the Karbon Practice Excellence survey, you'll see references throughout the book, providing key facts and substantiation to the theory and solutions we recommend. More information on the survey is available on the book's website.

The Journey to Enterprise Value

Our book is centered on the most important resource in any service organization: human capital. Employee salaries and benefits are typically 50 percent or more of overall costs in running our service organizations. Because our firms are based on knowledge work, that expenditure makes sense, but a well-run organization is required to maximize its value.

Our book is going to walk you through all the facets of managing your organization, including what managing capacity means for you, how to manage scaling plateaus at various team sizes, and what the role of the firm owner and entrepreneurial leader must become. Part One will speak to the firm's leadership, team management, team dynamics, firm culture, organizational behavior, and organizational design. Part Two will focus on various types of capacities, their constraints and complexities, and how to calculate capacity planning. Part Three will focus on the operational aspect of your firm, explaining operations management, both strategically and tactically, to ensure proper execution and planning from the strategic decisions in the first two parts. Finally, in the last chapter we wrap up the book by showing how it all comes together to create your global maximum enterprise value. And for a bit of foreshadowing, we can let you know that (a) bigger isn't better and (b) profitability is king and queen.

In a sentence, this book is about scaling your service organization on purpose. Growing your firm can't be done accidentally. If you are not intentional about scaling, you will hit the plateaus and walls that could hinder you, slow you down, and even completely dismantle your organization's value and ability to exist. You will see that with intention comes the work necessary to build your company well. We'll walk you through the recipes that firms like Jade Consulting and 3 Media Web leveraged to leap forward, and you'll see what you need to do to build the service organization of your dreams.

And if, after reading our book, you still feel overwhelmed, then check out the book's website, scalewithpurpose.info. Many of the resources included in this book are available there. You'll also find live Scaling Workshops you can attend, as well as the opportunity to hire us for consulting, engage us to speak to your group, or invite us to join you on a podcast or webinar. We dedicated the time to write this book to make sure you have what you need to scale your service organization with purpose. Welcome to the journey.

PART I

LEADERSHIP

&

CULTURE

1

What You Signed Up For

We grew very quickly. Within a year,
we doubled the team, which had always been
a flat hierarchy. And I remember when we
reached 16 employees, Heather, the owner, said,
"I think this is enough. Let's not go any further."

ANTONIYA BEYRIYSKA
(PRACTICE MANAGER OF ASK THE BOSS;
8 EMPLOYEES)

FOUNDED TWENTY-ONE years ago in London, employee-owned Ask the Boss is one of the more progressive accounting firms in the world and has won numerous awards along the way. With a long tradition of serving amazing clients, Ask the Boss provides superior client service and world-class advisory services. As Antoniya says:

> If a client needs something urgently, they are always welcome to communicate with someone else from the team. We are a bit like the back office for our clients. That's why initially our company was called Back Office Support Solutions (now BOSS), because of the soft touch services that we offer.

But, as for many firms, the goal in time shifted to growth—in terms of revenue, clients, and headcount. In 2019, Ask the Boss grew from 8 to 16 employees, doubling in less than a year. However, the growth conflicted with the mission, culture, and structure. Things ground to a halt:

> We were signing up clients and employees on a weekly and monthly basis. Everyone was overworked, and we started seeing lots of problems with our client service. It felt really disheartening because the people involved were doing hard work, going the extra length to spend additional hours to train, onboard, and shadow new team members, while our clients were telling us that they felt that we let them down. We just couldn't sustain the rapid growth.

Heather (the owner) and Antoniya (the practice manager) knew this wasn't what they wanted or had signed up for. So they made the painful decision to downsize and return to where they operated optimally—8 employees. As Antoniya told us:

> It became much easier to manage the practice with fewer people and fewer problems. And at this moment, we're pretty much on the same level of revenue generation that we were when we were 16 people. We are very happy with where we are at. I remember back when I started nine years ago in the company and Heather said to me, "I never want to grow the business more than 10 people because this is the happiest place I could ever be."

Can You Have It All?

Jason Blumer

Like every entrepreneur out there, I once chased the dream of "having it all." But here's a truth I learned the hard way: You can't have it all—at least not all at once.

As founders, we launch our firms pursuing freedom—breaking away from constraints to build something on our terms. It's this very pursuit of unfettered freedom that often becomes our biggest downfall while scaling our businesses. It certainly was for me.

You might be thinking, "What's he talking about? My firm is doing great!" And perhaps it is right now. But I can guarantee: What works for your service organization today won't work as you scale. When you add more revenue, bring on more team members, and deliver increasingly complex services, everything changes. It must, and we'll show you why in this book. That complete freedom you're expecting to find once you hit a certain size of revenue or when you've finally built a team of smart people with a lot of experience? Freedom is not waiting for you there.

If you're looking to scale your services company as your path to freedom, you need to start with some fundamental questions:

- What kind of business do you actually want to lead?

- What's the real goal of your organization? (And what's your personal goal?)

- Do you want what it means to scale your organization?

That last question—that's the one my business partner Julie Shipp hit me with years ago. It was a wrecking ball (delivered with love) that I didn't like hearing. At the time, I was unknowingly dismantling my business—drowning in debt, behind on taxes, with my personal relationships crumbling. Julie had just joined as my partner to help me turn things around when she heard me say on a podcast, "I'm done. I just want to go mow grass for a living." She was, understandably, not thrilled.

We had a serious conversation in which she asked me what I genuinely wanted. That started me on a multi-year journey of confronting my fears, addressing my immaturities, getting counseling, cutting my own salary, and climbing out of debt. That's when the truth hit me: You can't have it all. And that's when I truly began to understand what leading a scaling service organization means. I had to grow up. Through my partnership with Julie, I learned everything about what it really takes to lead a service business. We all need someone we can lean on, grow with, and learn from along this journey. Julie did that with me, and now we are relaying those truths to you in this book.

The leader of the service organization brings the realities of bridging the human team over to the design of the organization. For good or ill, the leader holds it all together. As we all start our careers in service entrepreneurship, we don't often see what it will take to hold a growing organization together. Most service entrepreneurs begin as the technicians who provide the actual service to the clients. But this must change over time. The service founder/owner must transition to being the business owner and operator, and move away from being the technician, if the business is to grow beyond themselves. This is difficult for all of us. Expect some personal growth ahead as you scale your service organization.

Do You Want What It Means?

Julie heard me say a number of times, "I want to grow!" while my actions displayed the opposite of what it actually means to grow. Heather and Antoniya learned similar lessons and came to realize what it means and what they wanted from their firm too. We all have to learn these same lessons if we are to be entrepreneurial leaders. So I'm asking you: *Do you want what it means to intentionally scale your organization?*

You can't just voice that sentiment; you have to sign up for what it means. And to be sure, *all* of our decisions, personal or professional, come with "what it means." There is no great journey you will sign up for or achievement you will enjoy in life that doesn't come with a decision and commitment to be and stay on that journey (for good or bad).

Maybe a better first question is this: Do you *know* what it means? But of course, that's why you're holding this book. If you don't know yet, you're going to. And we are beginning that journey by inviting you along in this first chapter to be the leader we know you can be. So, this is the first thing you have to do as the leader of your organization: decide that you want whatever it means to scale your organization. You must decide to do it—you can't accidentally stumble into scaling a service organization. As the title of this book implies, you must have a purpose. It has to be intentional.

A couple of years ago, at our global conference, I shared the definition of an entrepreneur with the audience. Entrepreneurs

- identify value in a market that represents unmet needs for users or clients;

- look into the future to meet those needs with intense curiosity;

- are willing to take risks (bets) on the future to create that value from an identified need;

- try, iterate, learn, and start or (re)start again if necessary; and

- apply past learning and mistakes so that they get better at taking risks in the future.

Now may be the time to ask yourself if you are the entrepreneur it will take to scale your organization. Do you align with the patterns we've seen in the entrepreneurs we've worked with? Do you want what it means? If you can be that entrepreneur, the world needs you. Our professional technical industries rely on technicians who turn into entrepreneurs to make our world economies work.

But before we get too inspirational, we want to make clear that you know you don't *have to* scale your organization, right? Many successful service-organization owners run "lifestyle" businesses. We call this "Hobbyist" and "Simple by Design" in our Entrepreneur's Mindset Matrix (shown later). This means the firm owners must keep their organizations small enough to let their personal lifestyle be their priority. There's nothing wrong with that, but you have to intentionally stay small too. It takes a lot of planning, but it can be done, and it requires only a few team members. If a lifestyle business is what you want, then you must decide to do that and accept what it comes with. The worst thing you can do is what I did: I tried to scale while holding onto the desire for a lifestyle firm and my broken pursuit of freedom the whole time. Heather and Antoniya learned that same painful lesson as well. I'm telling you now: A scaling service organization and a lifestyle business are two different things, and they do not sit together. So now is the time to decide what you want. This book is for those who *do* want to scale.

To be clear, while the question of whether you want to scale or drive a lifestyle business may be relatively simple, the path of entrepreneurship isn't an easy or linear one. The mindsets you have, the decisions you make, the people you hire, and the roadblocks you overcome will dictate the places you'll go. Fortunately, there is a looking glass into this that can prepare you for this challenging journey. We call it the Entrepreneur's Mindset Matrix, which Ian will show you in a moment.

Throughout the book, we'll dive deep into certain areas, like the matrix, to give you more context, insight, and tools while on your journey. While I have been consulting with and mentoring firms and owners of service organizations for decades and building my own firm for close to twenty-five years, Ian, my co-author, has been studying, analyzing, and instructing firm entrepreneurs how to run successful firms for just as long. When we deep dive, he'll be providing his decades of research work to demystify the journey.

As an added bonus, with each of us having over thirty years of experience in our careers consulting, coaching, and mentoring service firm entrepreneurs, we have each developed numerous ebooks, guides, frameworks, templates, and more. Where we can, we'll incorporate them throughout the book and point you to valuable resources you can access that exist outside the book. And you can always find out more on the book's website.

The Pathways of Scaling Firms

Ian Vacin

Since the early 2000s, working at Intuit, Xero, and now my own company, Karbon, I have been studying the nuances and intricacies of small businesses in the service sector, and more specifically across the accounting industry. From my early days in this journey, I've run many research studies, and I'm still doing it today to understand companies, their entrepreneurs, and what drives success and failures. From that research, we have been able to develop the Entrepreneur's Mindset Matrix (EMM), which provides a roadmap of how firms traverse the first scaling plateau, between 8 and 20 employees.

The Entrepreneur's Mindset Matrix

	Satisfied	Calculated	Entrepreneurial
0–1 FTE	Hobbyist	Just Starting	Idea on a napkin
2–7 FTE	Simple by Design	Simply Growing	Dreaming Big
8–20 FTE	Further growth requires formal processes	Efficient & Effective	Onwards & Upwards
20+ FTE		Mature & Traditional	Next Big Thing

As Jason mentioned earlier, it all starts with deciding whether you want what it takes to scale a firm. But while the basic choice may seem simple, your journey to get there is more complicated. Fortunately, it starts with you—the service entrepreneur—and your underlying, evolving mindset.

From the research, we've learned that your pathways depend on how you view your firm from two vantage points: satisfaction and growth. Among other things, we can narrow down where you sit in these mindsets from the following three questions:

- Satisfaction: How satisfied are you with how your business is performing?

- Past growth: What was your revenue growth percentage last year?

- Future growth: What do you expect your revenue growth percentage to be next year?

When answering the satisfaction question, you are classified as either high or low. For the growth questions, we take the difference between the growth percentages you provide, benchmark them against the responses of other business owners (from your industry sector), and classify your growth-mindedness as either high, medium, or low. To try it for yourself, take the quick survey on the book's website.

When combining the two variables, we discover three primary mindsets for service entrepreneurs:

Type 1 Satisfied (high satisfaction, low growth): Content, level-headed, and comfortable. Driving a lifestyle business, possibly part-time, with little to no desire to grow.

Type 2 Calculated (high satisfaction, medium to high growth): Realistic, confident, and collected. Understands where the business is at, looks realistically at where it can go, and sets short-term goals to get to the next level; mindset sometimes dictated by the constraints of the specific industry of the service entrepreneur (e.g., professional services).

Type 3 Entrepreneurial (low satisfaction, high growth): Ambitious, aggressive, and optimistic. Growth-minded and confident, and typically has prior experience or a strong team (rather than relying on luck).

Which mindset are you? When you combine the size of your firm (in employees) with your current mindset, you can see what type of firm you have today and where you can go from here. If you have a Calculated mindset and 6 employees (full-time equivalents, or FTEs), then you are in the "Simply Growing" category. If your mindset stays the same and your firm doubles in size, then you'll evolve to the "Efficient & Effective" category. In our survey of service founder/owners, 50 percent identified as Entrepreneurial, 40 percent Calculated, and 10 percent Satisfied.

In the EMM, you will notice two locations that aren't like the others. For those with the Entrepreneurial mindset, when it is just the founder or a set of co-founders (solo to 1 employee), this firm typically moves quickly into building ("Dreaming Big") without spending much time when they have their "idea on a napkin." For those with the Satisfied mindset, the journey becomes typically unenjoyable once the size of the firm requires formal management structures (more than 7 employees), and thus they stay smaller (fewer than 8 employees). Or they consciously move from a Satisfied to a Calculated mindset and add the necessary firm scaffolding around processes and management, moving quickly into an "Efficient & Effective" firm. We'll discuss this later in Chapter 3.

You will notice that there are no arrows in the EMM. This is because you won't necessarily travel from one mindset to the next. Your journey, and your firm's journey, isn't always linear. For some readers, their mindset stays the same and their firm grows steadily in time, resulting in a progression down the EMM chart. Others hit unexpected turbulence, disruptions, life events, and scaling plateaus. These can change their trajectories, sometimes moving them backwards in employee headcount or across the matrix due to a changing mindset. It's okay to change mindsets; you just want to be aware of what is happening so you can respond in your scaling journey.

You might have noticed a gap in the matrix. What about the situation when the founder has low satisfaction and medium to low

Adversity is often a necessary ingredient in achievement.

DR. THOMAS SOWELL

———————————

growth-mindedness? This defines our last type, a sub-type of the Entrepreneurial mindset (not shown in the EMM):

Type 4 Overwhelmed (low satisfaction, medium to low growth): All over the place, struggling, and shaken. Strives to be Entrepreneurial, but lacks experience or know-how and tends to be involved in everything.

The Overwhelmed mindset doesn't exist at solo to 1 employee, since there are no results to shift this person away from their high growth-mindedness. It also doesn't exist at over 20 employees, as this mindset over time leads many firms to their death. The Overwhelmed mindset exists at 2 to 7 employees (we would call this "Hardly Simple") and 8 to 20 employees ("Struggling to Scale"). Typically, the scaling plateau experienced between 8 and 20 employees either causes a change of mindset or accelerates the firm toward its demise. As a result, the Overwhelmed mindset is a dangerous offshoot of the Entrepreneurial mindset. From our survey results, 78 percent of service founder/owners who identify as Entrepreneurial also self-select as Overwhelmed.

Before you panic: If you are labeled as a particular mindset today, this can, should, and will evolve over time. Are you where you want to be? Are you heading where you want to go? That is entirely up to you. There is nothing wrong with being a "Simple by Design" firm living the lifestyle dream. On the other hand, if you are in a "Struggling to Scale" firm, you are in a difficult position between ongoing frustration (stagnation leading to firm death) and rebuilding (downsizing)—but you can see where you are headed and how you, and the firm, need to change. If you take the time to reflect and act intentionally, you can move to a different category and even a different mindset in the EMM.

Now that we've given you a mental model to benchmark where you are at in your growth journey, let's talk more about you. As the leader of your service organization, you are fully responsible for the growth of your organization and the management of your team's capacity. So let's begin by dispelling the rumor that you can "hire experienced leaders and finally get a break." That may come over time in some sense, but you can't always delegate *all* of the duties of leadership. The higher-level duties of leadership will always be on your plate as the founder and/or owner as you grow (until you hand the firm off to someone else). To be sure, as you bring in more leaders over time, you get to delegate some of your leadership duties. But the assumption that you can hire someone and then *not* lead your firm is a misguided belief, and it can get you into trouble as you scale.

In fact, we see this reality play out in our Practice Excellence (PE) data, which we mentioned in the introductory chapter of the book. In our survey data, we quantified priorities by four variables: efficiency, strategy, growth, and management. The scores for the variables and the PE composite score are numbers between zero and 100 percent that indicate a firm's competency as compared to its peers. The median composite score value is 51.5 percent, so a score higher than that indicates that an entrepreneurial owner is more competent than the median of the firm owners in the sample. When you start your firm as a service entrepreneur, your strategy is your number-one priority and is the highest-scoring input variable in the composite score (55 percent). As your firm grows to be 2 to 5 people in size, efficiency quickly overcomes your strategy focus (growing from a baseline PE score of 53 percent to 56 percent). As you get even larger, management increases sharply in importance (largest percentage of growth for firms scaling between 2 and 50 people in size, going from 48 percent to 56 percent in PE score).

What Is a Service Organization?

Jason Blumer

Before we keep going, I want to define some language around the words "service" and "human." Economists generally refer to the service sector of our economy to differentiate it from the manufacturing sector, reflecting how the economies of the West changed in the twentieth century. Western economies have become more focused on services than on product manufacturing. This book is about the service sector, but our view for this book is narrower still.

A "human organization" is an organization focused on the production of knowledge-based "thought" deliverables, generally led by people with technical skills like accounting, legal, engineering, architecture, consulting, and design. Another word we could use to describe the leaders who should be reading this book is "professionals." These professionals may not all have some type of licensure, but they do all produce knowledge-based thought deliverables.

Why is this important to distinguish? Embedded in these human organizations are three key parameters that make it particularly challenging for you to manage the capacity of yourself and these types of professionals.

1. The founder/owners typically started out as technicians. They gained their experience through providing the technical services that they sell to their marketplace. As we have consulted with these organizations for many years, we have seen that it is difficult for a technical founder to become an entrepreneur scaling a business (which is why we wrote this book). Many questions come out of this truth:

- Who do you promote to leadership positions and why?

- What does it mean to review and/or lead the production of the technical work?

- What types of services can you sell to a market that is seeking technical deliverables?

2. The professionals working in the organization are technical too. This means there is a technical component to the deliverables that clients and customers are paying for. In a sense, your firm's capacity is limited by its ability to deliver technical outcomes quickly (doing this quickly means you will be more profitable). Technical knowledge often takes research, experience, and problem-solving, so technical knowledge is necessarily slow to arrive at these outcome deliverables. Delivering technical knowledge often requires multiple layers of review, since the delivery is expected to be technically accurate. So, the business model must support that expected value from the marketplace being serviced. Also, you can't just hire anyone you want to join your team, which makes capacity management more difficult. Your team is not generally interchangeable with other employees, because they have specialized technical abilities. Tim Williams, author of *Positioning for Professionals*, calls these organizations professional knowledge firms, which is a great summary of these types of organizations.

3. Knowledge is the deliverable. You may say "duh," but this fact can cause a lot of problems in the capacity management of your human organization. Knowledge is invisible. It can't be seen or held, and it's often difficult to even know when it's been created or delivered. Knowledge flowing through your professional organization must be priced high enough, scoped well, documented in a workflow system, provided on time, captured and notated, collected for, and ultimately delivered all in a profitable way. Knowledge is what you sell, but it's hard to see, scope, and deliver.

Ian and I run service organizations, and we have for a long time. We too struggle with all of these issues. We also consult with organizations to solve these complex problems because they are hard to know anecdotally. As we begin, we want to convince you that scaling a professional service organization, a human organization, is more complicated than most people realize. If you start off with the wrong belief, then you'll struggle when times get hard. We hear it often in the complaints from our consulting clients: "Why won't my team just do what they are supposed to do?!" This just shows the misguided view many leaders of human organizations have about growing their organization. Don't be surprised when things don't hum like you expected. Your team needs to know what to do, and how, before they can do it.

Firm Size Is the Leader's Responsibility

Headcount is a choice, not an outcome; choose the number you can lead well.

CHAD DAVIS
(CO-FOUNDER OF LIVECA; 60 EMPLOYEES)

Chad Davis gets the complexity of scaling a human organization. He and his co-founder, Josh Zweig, began scaling one of the first remote and virtual professional accounting firms in Canada. They are the OGs, and they grew rapidly. Chad is a strategic and insightful mind in the accounting profession. His firm is value driven and profitable, with a strong culture. Both Chad and Josh have been very calculated in how they run and operate the firm, making sure employees and clients are happy. Their tale, which we will dive into at a couple of points in the book, is one of struggle going through multiple scaling plateaus and deciding ultimately that employee size is only one important determinant of firm success. They grew rapidly up to 120 team members, and then learned the ultimate size of their organization through the path of the pandemic. They intentionally shrank down to around 60 team members, their optimal size. Chad and Josh learned that firm success was about reducing complexity, maximizing employee engagement and satisfaction, ensuring client deliverable quality (and happiness), and creating predictable profit, all in a newly designed business model, and all while staying true to the company's mission and core values.

Shrinking a firm may not sound like a win, but as you'll see, strategic and intentional shrinking can be a win, and it was one for LiveCA. The key is that they consciously optimized their size. They saw a problem, and they did something about it. And that is what you should always be doing as the leader. You are fully responsible for the strategy of your organization, its subsequent growth, and the management of the team. And you will always have to deal with what leading and scaling a human organization comes with. You *cannot* delegate the overarching strategy of capacity and growth to anyone else (unless they become part of the leadership team or owners).

Just like Chad, if you are a leader of a human organization, then you are probably struggling in some way. For entrepreneurial leaders, your approach, style, and thinking evolve over time as you mature and learn how to lead different sizes. You'll learn valuable and painful lessons as you scale. Human organizations are living things and evolve over time typically as the entrepreneurial leader also evolves and matures. When the organization hits growth points (akin to teething, teenage years, etc.), things don't feel, look, or operate like they used to. Projects take longer, efforts to complete tasks feel harder, teams don't respond and work like you thought they would when you hired them, and it becomes harder to grow profitably. For an entrepreneur, that is to be expected, but it is frustrating, nonetheless. You may be failing at times, but that's okay. It's part of the journey.

The firm that you built must evolve. The strategy must change as the size, your market, and the economy changes. Heck, the people might need to change, and you will change too as you get older. When we look at the Practice Excellence research, firm owners continue to focus and refine their strategic competencies for at least five years (the overall PE score for strategy increases from 53.5 percent to 54.5 percent) until they feel confident in their strategic direction and purpose (by which point the overall PE score for strategy falls to 51.8 percent due to complacency).

Where are you on that journey? To be sure, what brought you success a few years ago won't be the strategy that will help you succeed in the coming years. You may miss your targets, which means you'll miss opportunities. This is very frustrating because it will slow down and inhibit your growth as an organization. Ultimately, missing targets is about a lack of strategy evolution in your organization (something we will explore in depth in this book). The degree by which your targets were missed is further exacerbated by whether the firm was properly measuring the targets and inputs in the first place. The lack of active measurement of your targets (you know, the ones you keep missing) causes the problem to fester, and the negative impact compounds in layers on top of the previous years' missed targets.

As a leader, then, you must set the strategy, evolve the strategy, decide the targets of your growth, empower the team, measure whether you are achieving your targets, course correct when necessary, and do this all in a profitable way over time as you evolve. And there is no telling what you are going through personally while doing all of this. This is hard! We're being direct with you, but you have to hear the truth: You are responsible as the leader. Once you embrace this truth and dry your tears, you can grow—and even define growth—in a more methodical and strategic way.

The Service Team Is Also the Leader's Responsibility

You are not only responsible for the strategy, growth, and capacity management of your service organization. You are also responsible for your team. If you struggle as the leader, typically your team will struggle in kind. A struggling team in a service organization means we can usually look to leadership and see where they have failed to prioritize work, clearly define roles, and call a team back to the organization's culture. Teams need engagement, clarity, goals, and tools, and they need to feel the weight of their roles as they are called to participate in the organization's mission. This is the leader's job as they care for their team, if capacity management is ever to become a focus of the service organization.

Your expectations of yourself as an entrepreneurial leader can't be the same as your expectations of your team members. You signed up for something very different than your team. For you, it is your life savings, your livelihood, your ego and pride, your dreams and opportunities. For your team, it might be everything from "just a job" to "my dream company." With that said, you need to work with your team to motivate them for the role they have taken, incentivize them with their pay, inspire them through your actions, and use input measures for the accountability they need to bump their work up against. You can't improve what you don't measure, and that goes for measuring your own capacity first.

Leaders do the important work of caring for their human team by creating a strong culture. Does your organization feel "loose"? A strong culture tightens up an organization as it grows. Cultural adherence for the team is the tight, focused, and structured way you invite the team to work in your organization. A result of this type of culture is accountability. Do you want your team to feel more accountable? Then design, maintain, and—as needed—change your culture deliberately.

One of my mentors, Peter Block, defines accountability in a counterintuitive way, and one Ian and I agree with. Block says a team becomes accountable by being *invited* into a role and an organization and by agreeing to the commitment required of them—which is what they sign up for with employment in your organization. In this view, accountability is expected and assumed because of the employment commitment the team member made when they accepted the job. Accountability to the culture of your organization comes from within the team member and can be assumed to exist from the owner's perspective. Therefore, Block says, you can't "hold" anyone accountable to anything.

Instead of compliance, Block speaks of commitments the team members make when they accept the job:

- Instead of forcing people to do something they don't want to do, leaders must create organizations that promote ownership from within the team member.

- Instead of holding people accountable, leaders must call them to participate in something they want, then work collaboratively under the commitment the leader and team member have made together.

Of course, as leaders we do have to be clear about what we need the team to be doing every day. When you set accountability correctly inside of a tight culture, you allow the right team to feel the weight of their role and the responsibility they agreed to when they took the job. "Making" and "forcing" accountability leads to parent-child dynamics, according to Block, and this inhibits the initiative and genuine responsibility that team members should hold. You can learn more about Block's views in a podcast I did with him in March 2022, which we've linked to on the book's website. Peter Block's book, *The Answer to How Is Yes*, also addresses some of these foundational concepts.

So, a strong, tight culture of responsibility is one of mutual commitment and shared purpose. The leader brings the purpose, and the team brings the commitment. Both are required.

Normally when we discuss purpose, vision, mission, and values, it gets confusing. Let's quickly define what each term means:

Your purpose, or your "why," is your polarizing beliefs. These are beliefs you'll stand on, even at the risk of financial loss. You could ask, "What am I willing to lose in commitment to my purpose?" The purpose typically starts with the words, "We believe…."

Your vision can be aspirational, and it is what you create when you ultimately realize your purpose. That is, your vision is what you will commit to bring into this world through your business, knowing you may fail. It takes courage to have a vision, but the organization and team desperately want it. The vision typically starts with, "We will…."

Your mission is a practical place you want to embody in your marketplace. You are seeking to be different in your mission, not just better. Tim Williams says, "Being good at what you do isn't all that's required to achieve real greatness; you must devote just as much effort to being different." It is an ambitious yet achievable position in your clients' lives that recognizes your purpose. It typically starts with, "Be the most…."

Your values are your five to seven core-principle statements that you can wash over your team on a weekly basis, reminding them of the culture you've invited everyone to work in. They are written in your company's voice and provide the guidance needed on how to work together as a team and with your clients. They typically are a few words long and can start with a verb.

Who holds all of these pieces together? It's the leader and their commitment to the care of their service team.

Take Courage

As a leader of a human organization, you've signed up for a highly complex task that will change you and certainly must continually change your organization. It's no wonder that you've tripped up or that you will trip up again. It's no wonder that the journey feels daunting, confusing, and unknown most of the time. As I've gotten older and my three kids have left the nest, I realize now that my parents didn't know what they were doing most of the time. Neither do I. Running a business is very similar.

As a leader, you may not always know what you are doing, but there is a path forward, and we're going to show you. We'll show you how to tighten your organization up so that it can scale (if you want it to), how to avoid the biggest mistakes, and what to do when you make them. You are a leader, so you have a responsibility, and you can't just assume your human organization will operate without you. Remember, we lead human organizations full of humans. We're human too, and we don't always know what we're doing, even if our team doesn't know that.

Your part is to accept what it means to be a leader, and with that comes leaning into your team, not away from them. As the leader, you are responsible for the care of your organization and team. Take courage. You can do this—and we're going to show you how.

2

More Than Just Billable Hours

The only people who track time are inmates.
BERNARD ACKERMAN, CPA
(PRESIDENT AND OWNER OF BNA; 48 EMPLOYEES)

I've got a simple rule. You just gotta book
every minute to your timesheet.
ZANE STEVENS, CA
(FOUNDER AND PARTNER OF PROTEA FINANCIAL; 40 EMPLOYEES)

AN HAS KNOWN both Bernie Ackerman (BNA) and Zane Stevens (Protea Financial) for almost ten years. Both accounting firms are some of the most progressive in the United States and have grown quickly through the scaling plateaus that many firms struggle with. But they stand on opposite ends of the major debate for service firms: to track time or not to track time.

Bernie founded and oversees BNA, which is now almost fifty years old and a regional powerhouse. His firm appears from the outside to be traditional, as most employees come to the office located in Rock Hill, South Carolina. But don't be fooled: Bernie is one of the pioneers in value pricing. He feels that tracking time isn't productive because the value is baked in when providing a proposal to the client. And because he runs a very efficient organization, tracking time for the purposes of understanding productivity isn't needed:

> Productivity is measured by revenue recognition. We look at the annual revenue managed and the number of tasks per employee. We hire professionals and give them the freedom to get the work done in the way they want to get their job done. What matters is what revenue you bring in, not how well you can lie on your timesheet.

Zane founded Protea Financial over ten years ago, and the firm focuses on accounting for the wine industry. The company has grown over 50 percent in both revenue and headcount over the past three years. Although Zane lives in Novato, California, he oversees a fully distributed team, with most employees reporting out of Northern California and South Africa. He uses time tracking not for punishment but rather to ensure people aren't overworked and that the firm hires at the right time:

> How can you know your team's productivity without knowing where they are spending their time? You can't optimize what you don't measure.

Two very successful service organizations with two very different perspectives. However, both leaders value time and use it to drive maximum profitability for their firms.

The Human Element

Jason Blumer

Any professional service firm, or any organization that produces "thought deliverables" in exchange for money, is a *human* organization. Pair the fickleness of the human employee with delivering services within processes and deadlines and the result is often fraught with misalignment and confusion. When—and only when—you understand the realities of humans can you manage your organization's output, protect its market position, and scale it profitably.

Humans have free spirits and their own minds, so when you invite them into your organization to follow your purpose, vision, and the values you believe in, you are asking them to set aside their own beliefs about how to achieve success. In that sense, the humans who work for you don't even have the same goal as you. You may be building a valuable company that seeks to make a profit, while your employees may be looking for a safe place to work with their expertise, enjoy their work in your culture, feel safe, and make money for themselves and their families. As an entrepreneur, you may want to expand through chaos, while a new employee may feel they have finally found a place they can settle in safely after the chaos of a previous job.

In our exploratory research and interviews, we found that over 90 percent of firm owners prioritize employee engagement over customer satisfaction or firm profitability. Perhaps this hyper-focus on employees is in response to the potential misalignment between the owner and the team. You can begin a relationship with an employee with a level of misalignment that may come out only later, when you ask the team to do things the way you want them done (while setting aside their own beliefs about how things should be done).

Shockingly, your employees have their own ideas about how your company should operate. As a leader, you are wise to listen to them; yet only you can make the decisions about how your company produces its deliverables and protects its market value. This is your reality if you own a growing service organization. Great leaders are empathetic and listen to their teams, yet they must also decide how professional capacity will be used, delivered, priced, and paced through their organization. If you haven't clearly established how your team's commitment will be turned into profit and taught your team how to do it, your organization will struggle.

We've already seen that it begins with the foundational purpose of a culture, but it extends to practical aspects too, like the design of the organization, accountable processes, and consistent team training. In fact, from our Practice Excellence research, we've learned that the largest contributor to firm success is providing internal training to your employees. To be clear, your employees' job is to perform their work as laid out by the owner, and the owner's job is to say how things will be done in their organization. If you have not clearly defined expectations and allowed your team to work within accountable places, then no amount of thought or frameworks will allow your company to scale sustainably.

PROMISE

Promises to clients can come in the form of stated service principles: "We respond to emails within twenty-four hours"; "We deliver all financials on the fifteenth of each month." They can also be in the form of pre-booked meetings related to deliverables: "Our final design presentation will be the last Wednesday of this month—let's set that meeting up now." However you state a promise, we believe in making it overt and the value that comes from having made a promise to someone.

For example, service firms use deadlines to get their work done. This is to give a clear promise to the client and provide guardrails for the team to work in a balanced way. If in your company you allow deadlines to be missed or ignored or for the final delivery of that deadline to always fall on the owner's plate, then you are likely operating out of fear or some other dysfunction in the employer/employee relationship. Expecting the team to stick to deadlines, you may be fearful about giving the work back to a team member when they have not met the standard of the deliverable, fearful about making promises to the clients as to when they will receive their deliverables, or even negligent in setting up processes in the first place and following up on them with the team. Negligence in doing the work is often disguised as laziness on the part of the entrepreneur/owner.

As the owner, you have to face the fear of what clear leadership comes with. You need clear standards of operations and deliverables in your service organization for the team to see what they are shooting for, and also so you can make promises to the clients. Client promises are one way you can justify your initial request for a price, and the delivery on that promise is what proves your value. Humans make promises and carry the weight of that responsibility for the good of everyone involved in the relationship. In our Practice Excellence survey results, most of the overwhelming majority of top-quartile firms have standard operating procedures and set operating mechanisms that fuel their Practice Excellence score, revenue per employee, and overall growth. If you're afraid to set standards and, as a result, don't have a consistent culture of accountability, your organization will gradually decline as it slogs through the many personal preferences and lenses everyone wears in their professional work.

Right-Brained? Left-Brained?

Though neuroscience has largely dismissed the concept that right-brained people are creative and left-brained people are analytical, it's a great mental model for discussing the difficulty we face in scaling a human organization. As a firm gets larger in revenue production and team size (two key constraints to monitor in scaling), we can label the people as right-brained and the structure and processes as left-brained. One is creative and has ideas, and one provides the foundation to the structure.

I believe all people are creative and have their own predetermined will as to what they like and dislike and what they prefer to do and ignore. As an organization grows larger, the structure to support that larger company comes with more processes, workflow tools, policies, and cultural protocols for everyone to follow. The creative human who works for you may not always want to follow the structure you put in place. "This place is stifling!" they may say. This relationship with structure and freedom can become a growing problem as the firm continues to scale and asks for more adherence from the creative humans to the structure being implemented. Some team members embrace ever-added structure (Ian did), while some push back (I did). Some people use creativity as an excuse to ignore important structures. This problem can worsen as you continue to allow the team to "do what they want."

Service organization growth isn't linear. It's a series of plateaus. The strategies, organizational design, culture, and leadership that enabled a solo-to-5-person firm to be successful aren't the same as the structure that enables an 8-to-12, 15-to-25, and 30+-person service firm to be successful. Since growth in a service firm isn't linear, it means one growth plateau must end, while you have to begin a brand-new growth strategy to form a new trajectory. Like a firm's processes, its strategy and structure must undergo continuous improvement—and often disruption. We call this restructuring. Combined with the people and their creative ways of working, the right- and left-brained aspects of the firm can overcome the inherent team dynamic issues that create the plateaus of growth illustrated in the graphic below.

Scaling Plateaus

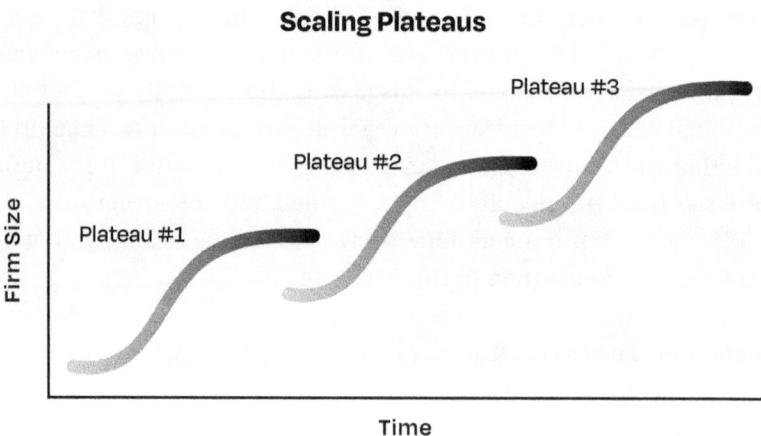

As the owner moves further and further away from technical revenue production and delivery and is unable to know the team on a one-to-one basis, the scaffolding provided by the structure takes the place of the owner's personal touch as they take on more and more revenue. (If you don't like this truth, don't scale your service organization.) In fact, the firm's systems and structure, as well as the team members' expertise, must mature as more revenue comes into the organization. The maturing of these systems and humans typically lags behind the increase in revenue. Entrepreneurs love to dump revenue into a firm (I do!), but they must also realize that this imposes on the agency's structure and people a need to mature at the same pace that revenue is being added. We'll take a deeper dive into revenue's role in scaling in Chapter 5.

Our data reinforces this need for more structure. In our Practice Excellence survey, the top two quartiles across all segment sizes show higher usage of key operating mechanisms (more scaffolding) than their lesser-performing counterparts. After an organization has grown larger, the team's weight of accountability can wane if its members don't also feel the weight of accountability through the scaffolding: the processes, deadlines, protocols, and workflow systems calling them to their work. Why is this? In human organizations, the humans always tend to migrate toward their own islands of thought and move away from accountability. As the firm grows larger, teams can hide more easily (even unknowingly). To counter this tendency in people, scaffolding replaces the presence of the founder/owner and reminds them of their commitment to the accountability required for them to remain engaged with the growing enterprise.

As mentioned earlier, we tell our team that their role has weight to it. We want our team to feel the weightiness of accountability that their role requires of them. Their role is heavy sometimes, which means it's valuable. With that accountability in place, we hope they can commit to what the company needs from them as it scales, which is a team that is willing to trust the leadership with the new structure being added as the company restructures over time. And that structure needs to be set explicitly and then enforced. A leader who says, "I don't care how the team gets their work done, as long as they deliver," leaves a wake of disorder and confusion and no defined process of delivery for the growing firm to be successful. People come with many different perspectives, backgrounds, and previous work experiences, and an open-ended invitation to work however they want can be interpreted in ways the owners never anticipated.

"Unlimited PTO" is also misguided. Obviously, personal time off (PTO) cannot by definition be unlimited, so stop saying things like that. It's just confusing. When a service organization is small (no more than 8 people), the owner is close to the team, knows well what team members are doing, and can respond quickly and effectively to their needs and troubles. But when a company grows, "the heavens are high and the emperor is far away." Without the owner's direct oversight, unlimited PTO can be abused and misused by weaker employees in a large organization—and it can also punish some good employees who, without the push of a "use it or lose it" PTO structure, don't take the time off they actually need to recharge.

You don't get to break your own rules, either. That's "playing against yourself," a concept my partner taught me many years ago. If you break your own rules, it gives others an excuse to disregard the processes and protocols your firm needs as it grows. As the owner, you have to be the best example of following the rules.

Even as we hear leaders voicing their desire to let the team do what they think is best, we hear these same leaders struggling with an "overwhelmed" team, inefficient work delivery, reverse delegation, employees quitting or covertly working multiple full-time jobs, firms being ghosted by new team members, virtual employees disappearing, not being able to hire competent teams, and more. Some of these issues can't be fixed. And some of these issues, and many more, are a result of an arbitrary, unintentional organization hoping that the team just "does the right thing."

The most caring leaders are the ones who are clear about the structure being added to the company as it grows. Teams need and want this; they just won't tell you. We are calling all leaders to do what's right for the organization, not what employees espouse as preferable. Caring leaders can take time to add scaffolding in this way:

1 Get the team's input on new policies, procedures, and newly proposed structure.

2 Introduce new standards with time for the team to give feedback.

3 Require feedback from the team (professionals always have feedback even if they say they don't, so you have to ask for it).

4 Tweak the structure with the feedback.

5 Ask the team to explicitly embrace these new structures for the good of the company, knowing some team members won't like the results.

You'll notice we don't ask for "buy-in" from the team. The only buy-in you as the owner need from your team is the exchange of their employment contract (their commitment) for the paycheck you give them (your commitment). Like accountability, buy-in can be assumed once they have been hired. Team members have opinions (which is why the list above includes seeking their input), but please stop seeking permission from a group of people you have hired to fulfill your mission. That is a fool's game, and it will get harder and harder as your organization grows.

Leaders need to see that their leadership and clear guidance is a gift to their team. Then the right team needs to focus their efforts on the success of their role and the mission of the service organization they work for. It's a collaboration between the employer and the employee. While you scale, give your team the gift of your leadership, and stop seeking their approval for doing what you know is right.

Tracking Time and Calendar Blocking

"Time is money," they say. Obviously, they're wrong. Time is important, sure, but there's a lot more to making money—and scaling a service organization profitably—than tracking time. As we already stated, we do know that this has been a consistent area of opinion and argument over the past thirty-plus years. When we spoke to value-pricing advocates like Bernie Ackerman, we heard things like, "People are just going to lie on a timesheet. If something isn't working, your team or clients will tell you—not a timesheet." And when we spoke to time-tracking advocates like Zane Stevens, we heard things like, "We use timesheets as a tool to make sure people are in a place where they're comfortable, they can give their best effort, and they can be successful. They ensure we have sufficient hours to cover the billable hours we have required on a monthly basis." We love both sentiments.

Many service organizations are growing wiser and seeking to produce their revenue through pricing as opposed to billing. For a simplistic explanation, "pricing" means deciding on your revenue with the client *before* you start the work, whereas "billing" is calculating your revenue by adding up all the time spent multiplied by an hourly rate *after* you have completed the work for the client. Though more modern firms don't bill for time, many still say, "We don't bill clients based on time, we just track time to make sure we know the right budgets to commit to our work." That statement implies that the service firm is regularly reviewing tracked time, adjusting the amount of budgeted time a team member can spend on client work, and also adjusting their prices with clients because they have learned from accurate time tracking that they under-priced a project. But even though they voice this specific value of time tracking, few firms use time-tracking data in this way.

When we surveyed service-organization owners on this, 94 percent agreed on the importance of time budgets, while only 62 percent used time budgets. Time budgets are prepared in advance as a prediction of the work that has been sold and a guide to the team producing the deliverables. Time tracking, from the

Fear is the mind-killer. Fear is the little-death that brings total obliteration. I will face my fear. I will permit it to pass over me and through me.

LADY JESSICA, IN *DUNE*, FRANK HERBERT

perspective of tracking productivity (rather than billing purposes), is tracking the actual work that can be compared to the budget.

We consult with many service organizations, and we find it is rare that firm leaders perform a regular historical analysis of effort input and subsequently adjust their team's output and the client's prices, based upon this supposed historical research. Our survey results show some interesting findings:

- 71 percent of firms surveyed use time tracking.

- 74 percent of firm owners trust the data that tracking time provides.

- Most firms (53 percent) review the data no more than quarterly.

- 33 percent of firm owners never review the data.

We're not trying to convince you to stop tracking time if you do, but we are suggesting you take an honest look at whether you're really using it for what you say you're using it for.

Over twelve years ago, in my accounting firm, we came to believe that time tracking was not effective, and we haven't tracked time since. That didn't come without its issues. I believe there are numerous reasons why time tracking is faulty. For example, it's a task imposed on employees that burdens their work requirements, the data is often unreliable (humans have faulty memories, so they key in inaccurate data from the past), and firms write their bills up and down based on emotional whims or market changes. We would certainly never rely on our team's past memory to produce our firm's revenue. But when we abandoned time tracking, we lost some methodology, albeit a faulty one, for creating our client invoices. So after I uninstalled the time billing system on our servers, we had to scramble quickly and figure out how we would ask for our money up front before we started work, now that we were thrown into the art of pricing.

We eventually began having our team prioritize their work in the form of hours for the upcoming week as a part of the work planning processes. Instead of tracking time from the past, we now attempt to predict our time as a firm for the upcoming week's calendar by having team members block a week in advance (essentially preparing their timesheets in advance). This idea came out of the calendar planning methodology my partner and I were using, called Strategic Calendar Work Blocking (SCWB). Planning our calendar a year in advance is a strategic behavior often reserved for leaders and owners, so our team's view and vision are typically just focused on the next week. And, of course, no one can actually predict what will happen a year in advance. On the book's website you can find podcasts that explain how we go through SCWB.

This change in blocking future time as opposed to tracking time spent in the past has created many unforeseen benefits that aid us in our efforts toward accurate capacity planning, providing the data we need to operate our scaling firm. Here are three key benefits we gained—we call these the 3 Ps of time blocking:

Prioritizing work. Prioritization is a capacity skill, but few have been taught this skill or practiced it over time in service organizations. A team may become overwhelmed because they weren't given clear deadlines or because they're trying to do more work than they actually have time to do. Proper capacity management requires a team to have an accurate view of what work to do next week and what to do in the weeks after that. Every team member perceives this differently, and it is management's responsibility to help the team prioritize the placement of their work clearly. We are to prioritize our professional work in light of the firm's goals, not based on the employee's whims. Even if a team member has space for work, there are often reasons why certain client work should be moved to a later time (for example, during times when a team member should be focused on their own professional development and education instead of client work). Keep in mind that your team members' choices of the work they prioritize affect the promises you are making to clients. It's all connected.

Planning work. Being able to look into the future and appropriately place different levels of work on a calendar is a skill. You as the owner struggle with this, as does your team. One skill for preparing work efficiently is batching (scheduling a large amount of work of the same type in the same calendar space). Batching is highly efficient, and a team member who is skilled at this (many are not) knows to put all of the same types of work in batched calendar blocks and match them to the way they prefer to work. For example, someone may know themselves well enough to do all the most technical work mid-morning and will plan their upcoming week accordingly. Or a manager, instead of scattering their meetings with teams and clients throughout the week, may batch them into just one day. This can greatly increase the efficiency of those meetings, as well as the efficiency of all of their work for that week.

Another detail of planning is time off. We require two weeks of planning for a team member to take time off. They lay out their plan for the time off, and we work collaboratively with them on how this will work with other team members and the clients.

A team member's ability to plan their work with the right priority, while also fulfilling all their personal commitments, means they will be a healthier person. This is not done in a vacuum: Planning is highly collaborative. It takes the employee and the owner working together to make sure the planned time is going to work. The owner does not have to carry the responsibility for the team member's personal upsets, life changes, and commitments. But the team member and the owner do have the responsibility to be honest and transparent with each other to make sure the plan fulfills the work commitment the team member has agreed to and to allow them time off to rest and refresh.

Predicting work. Prediction is also a skill to be learned by the team members who are blocking their calendars a week in advance. When a team attempts to block their calendar in advance, they are displaying the lens through which they are anticipating their upcoming work complexities, team and client needs, and personal requirements and the ups and downs of professional technical client service. A team member who predicts their calendar in consistently poor ways could be revealing an immaturity in knowing what their work requires of them. Poor prediction could also be a result of the leaders being unclear with the calculated budgets for the amount of time work will take, or a lack of self-discipline for the professional employee, or the leaders' inability or care to scope work appropriately for their team. The practice of predicting our work begins to reveal these faults.

Of course, no reflection of a professional team member's work is failproof. Tracking future predictions of work is a high-level skill, and a coach is needed to help the team along in their work. That can be provided by a skilled project manager. Project managers who have authority (that is, they hold a position of leadership on the team) can do a lot to help the team remain focused and stick to their calendar plan for the upcoming week, as well as help team members with planning and prioritization as the need arises.

Having a full team blocking their week ahead gives the leaders benchmarks to view when the team is struggling. When our team struggles (and we all do at times), we simply pull up the calendar and try to benchmark what they predicted with what actually happened. The delta between the two is what produces insights into their beliefs about work and our desires for efficient outputs. This comparison provides more concrete information to help team members better predict and plan for the upcoming week, and it shows us places where we were unclear about the budget predictions of the work.

One other side benefit of consistently looking at the week ahead is to emphasize in team members' minds their continual commitment to their role. We take employees' commitment for granted, but we shouldn't—a fact you will be reminded of when one surprises you with a resignation letter you weren't anticipating. Blocking a calendar a week in advance can help your team, and you, remember the valuable work they're called to do week after week.

Service versus Manufacturing

Ian Vacin

Many industries manage capacity planning for optimal efficiency and profitability. A look at manufacturing practices may be helpful for understanding the true realities of scaling a service organization with humans. Lean Manufacturing (we'll get to "Lean" in Chapter 9) seeks to create ultimate efficiency, with a streamlined manufacturing process where waste is continually eliminated. Therefore, manufacturing leaders seek to maximize efficiency and simultaneously eliminate waste. This methodology requires ongoing assessment to continually catch waste and eliminate it.

Some professional consultants compare Lean Manufacturing to professional service firms. This is a difficult comparison, since the whole makeup of service organizations is so different from that of manufacturing organizations. Kaizen is a Lean Manufacturing principle defined as the pursuit of perfection in manufacturing as a result of continuous improvement. Seeking any kind of perfection through continuous improvement is a great goal, but it is a real stretch for service organizations, where the team and leaders struggle in various seasons of life and the work of service organizations grows larger.

Lean Manufacturing tracks the uptime of operating machines. In a sense, the machines are more effective than their human operators in a manufacturing environment. Machines perform the output and make the money, so the machine is the focus. The humans' role is to keep the machine working at optimal performance. In a service-organization environment, on the other hand, the human is both the "machine" and the one causing the machine to operate at an optimal or suboptimal performance level. But of course, no human operates at an optimal level of performance, however you define that. They go through personal ups and downs. So, there is always some sense of "waste" (a manufacturing term) or inefficiency that we have to accommodate with our service teams. And service-organization leaders struggle too, just like their teams.

Another manufacturing concept often applied to service organizations is Six Sigma. Six Sigma, which we will also discuss in Chapter 9, is applicable to machine-based production systems, not human-based systems (although many concepts are transferable). People, like machines, have variances, up-time, and efficiency rates, but humans are more variable than machines. People go on vacation for a week or two (machines go down, but can typically be repaired quickly). People have good days and bad days, but the productivity on a bad day could be up to 50 percent worse than on a good day. People can extend their hours and productivity and become wildly more efficient if motivated for both good and bad reasons. It isn't that Six Sigma can't be applied to human-based systems; it is that your variances in a human-based system are larger and can't be planned for as easily. The purpose of Six Sigma is to understand variability in processes and resources and to work to mitigate those variances. The targets are different with humans.

A firm should seek to pursue efficiency through ordered systems for their teams, but teams aren't made of machines. Machines don't slack, blow off work, or get mad. Team members can quit, owners can lose interest, everyone can get distracted, and a team can simply ignore the processes and protocols you designed to help them work efficiently.

Remember, leader, you are the caregiver of the team and the organization. You sit in a place to view all that is happening with the team and the organization. As we've mentioned, you are the bridge that holds it together. You have to know the capacity of your team. Others can help you, give you insights, and provide you with metrics, but you really must know if your human team can fulfill the promises your organization is making to the market you serve. There's no point in just asking your team, "Do you have capacity for new clients?" They don't know. They think they know, but they don't sit at the level a leader does, so they can't see all the working parts (of which they are just one). They will answer that question through the lens of their own emotions and the weight they feel from their role in that moment, and from the perspective of their good or difficult week at home and their past experiences as an employee of all the places they have worked.

As the leader, you hold the human-based system together, recognizing the limitations of the humans (yourself included) and the promises you need them to fulfill to the clients. Hold on tightly to what is in your realm to own with your vision, which is the knowledge, design, and care of the humans that embody your organization's capacity. And delegate hard what the humans on your team should be doing—the revenue production. Embrace your role as leader of your growing human organization. We are going to help you do just that as we dive into practical aspects of designing your organization in the next chapter.

3

The Essential Blueprint for Success

When small and growing, you're taking the skeletons in the closet with you. Growth is what pushed us over the edge. Our original corporate culture was holding us back—we didn't have the right core values, right hiring processes, nor, ultimately, the right people.

DANIEL GERTRUDES
(FOUNDER AND CEO OF GROWTHLAB;
40 EMPLOYEES)

SCALING A SERVICE organization is tough—for everyone. GrowthLab, a full-service accountancy firm based in Providence, Rhode Island, is an example of innovation, progressiveness, and success. But success doesn't come easily, as Dan outlined. It takes a consistent focus and requires you, the entrepreneurial leader, to take ownership of the hard decisions.

After Dan purchased a 15-person firm, the flat, authoritarian organization he'd taken over just couldn't scale with the demand.

He had to fully restructure the firm from a flat structure to a hierarchical one to create more accountability, while putting the right people in the right seats to enable both revenue growth and a positive corporate culture. Dan recalls:

> I understand the power of leverage and what a world-class professional services business gross margin should look like. I used to sleep at night when my gross margins for accounting were between 50 and 60 percent. With a professional services firm, you can easily create a leveraged pyramid. You know exactly how many people a person can manage, and you know what the theoretical capacity is for a pod.

Dan, a product of the financial services industry, is very scientific in designing and operating his firm. He closely monitors key performance indicators (KPIs) for all of his departments using gross margin (GM) as his measurement of choice. A blended 60 percent GM is the target, with various departments ranging between 50 percent (accounting) and 70 percent (CFO advisory). As he explains:

> Our higher gross margin departments are driven by tech, data acquisition, and increased productivity of team members. The way you increase productivity while decreasing variability in the professional services business is through professional development, leveraging technology, and standard operating procedures.

GROSS MARGIN

For service organizations, gross margin typically equals revenue minus some technology costs, minus direct billable labor (and benefits), and minus contractor costs. Then all other operating fixed expenses would come out of the gross margin. The calculation and inclusion of margins varies wildly among different service entrepreneurs, so don't get hung up on comparing your gross margin to Dan's—or anyone else's. You may be talking about two different margins.

Over time, Dan's organizational structure has evolved to include a C-suite, customer success, revenue, marketing, HR, and production teams. However, as we've mentioned, scaling is hard no matter whether you are small or large. As Dan reached almost 50 employees, his GM dropped to 44 percent, while his year-over-year growth dipped from 44 percent to 16 percent. Again, it required him to change the structure, re-look at the corporate culture, and ultimately right-size to reset things where necessary:

> It was because of how we were being managed. It was a hodge-podge matrix, which makes accountability impossible. Since then, we've shrunk the team, implemented Gino Wickman's Entrepreneurial Operating System (EOS), and taken out some of the concentration risk that we had with some of our larger customers. Now, gross margins are back above 50 percent and EBITDA is at 25 percent (up 70 percent), and we are poised for low single-digit organic growth this year.

How to Herd Cats

Jason Blumer

You're bringing people—complex, fickle former strangers—together to commit to a single vision targeting a particular market while offering particular services. Welcome to herding cats. You know how you herd cats? You put down good boxes, and they get right into them. The good box for your herd of cats is your organization. The way you design your organization is an essential part of your success or struggles as you grow your firm. The organization is what connects the people serving and the clients receiving the service. If you're struggling in any way with the growth of your service organization, the answer is this: Design your organization better. We'll show you how.

As an organization grows, it begins to adopt its own needs. The needs of the owners fade into the distance as the organization takes on a life of its own. This truly surprised me when it happened with the companies I lead. Founders who hang on to their own personal preferences don't realize the organization will have competing goals as it grows larger.

Consider this: A founder of a service organization sees the company begin to produce substantial profit when the organization is small and beginning to grow. In response, the founder draws more and more money out of the business to support a personal lifestyle that is also growing. Over time, the larger service organization adopts a higher risk profile and then needs to do what healthy organizations do: reserve large cash reserves to protect against market disruptions, manage surprising team disruptions, navigate around losing large clients and failed expensive technology deployments meant to create efficiency, et cetera. Eventually, the owner will have to give up their preference to use the organization for their personal wealth building. If they don't, there will come a time when the organization falters and the owner will need to give some of that cash back.

This scenario is common and can take owners by surprise as they learn lessons like this the hard way. This is exacerbated in professional technical service organizations when the founders continue to produce most of the service deliverables and take all the money out as a result of their hard work. For sure, this feels justified, but remember that you are still scaling a business. The organization can struggle to scale as a result of poor organizational design. The organization and the founders who created the organization are decidedly not the same thing. This fact is less obvious when the organization is small, and it becomes painfully obvious once the organization has to detach from the owner and live the life it was meant to live.

I've lived these hard lessons. I'm telling you about them so you won't make the same mistakes I've made.

An Introduction to Organizational Design

In our research and consulting experience, we've found that service firms tend to grow in levels, or strata, by team size. At each team stratum size, they must change their organization or they will stall in their growth at what some people call growth ceilings, and we've called scaling plateaus. Their leaders implement different forms of structure at different sizes. Here is what we've found in Service Organizational Strata (up to 50 team members):

Flat stratum: solo to 7 team members. You don't need much structure at this size. The leader is close enough to the team to know what is really happening. At this size, the leader also provides a large amount of the service deliverables to the clients. This is the stratum where firm owners, if interested, attempt a "lifestyle" business.

Management stratum: 8 to 12 team members. This is where structure begins to become important. The owner (or owners) must make decisive moves to implement management at this stage or they will struggle through the first scaling plateau. The owner must also begin moving out of the technical service delivery or their involvement will later bog down the growth of the organization. At this stage, the owner is also still in a technical oversight review role, as well as participating in ever-expanding leadership duties.

Departmental stratum: 13 to 25 team members. At this size, knowledge management and documentation have become complex, and the knowledge-sharing and management capabilities of the organization need to be departmentalized so knowledge can become more specialized and roles can become more focused. Roles that remain too general (i.e., broad) at this stage, where a role has too many types of different specialties embedded in it, begin to bog down the technical professional. As a result, the prior role definitions inhibit the efficiency of the team members' work as the organization becomes more complex. This is the level at which you need to figure out your technical service, accountable processes, revenue pipeline, team training, and market focus on a client base. If you don't, you will struggle to grow, and with each added person, your future restructuring will become all that more painful to execute. A solo founder may need a partner at this stage, as there may be too much leadership work for one founding partner to do on their own.

Leadership stratum: 26 to 50 team members. Do you want to be fully out of the work of the deliverables that your organization is producing? This is the level at which you'll get to begin doing that. At this level, you'll need four to five solid key leadership positions covering vision (CEO), finance/metrics (CFO), team care/HR/trainer (CPO), operations/project management (COO), and sales/revenue (CRO). You will likely have started adding some of these positions in the previous strata. At this stage, you'll also need to be cognizant of the order in which you add these leadership roles. The CFO finance/metrics role may be one of the first roles you add, while the CRO sales/revenue role may be one of the last.

It is important to understand these principles of organizational design so that you as a leader can notice, dismantle, and redesign (aka restructure) around scaling plateaus. Scaling plateaus are often experienced because an organization has been inaccurately designed or mismanaged as it has grown to a particular size. With service organizations in particular, changes in the design of the roles and the organization must be made in order for your firm to grow. Don't add the roles in the upper Service Organizational Strata too early, but don't add them too late either. This will always be the balance you must maintain in the organization's design: the timing and order of the addition of structural role complexities. If you "just want to finally be out of the technical service" but your team is only four people, you're far too early. The organization is not yet large enough to justify replacing your technical knowledge with an expensive new management role. This also means it is way too early to hire a manager to "replace" you when you have only five people on your team. Stay focused on your work, and that time will eventually come.

A principle in growth management is to add additional layers of firm structure at the minimum levels of complexity necessary. That is, keep it simple until you just can't anymore. As an organization grows, complexity is added to *support the weight* of the organization's mission. You should seek to add more complicated structures only when they are required by growth and not before. And certainly, as a founder/owner you should never add complexity just to serve your own desire for a break, to take away your stress, or for any other personal feeling you want to relieve. Complex structuring always requires more management, and this can lower profit per employee. We'll dig into this in more detail in the next chapter.

We can see in the Practice Excellence results that as a firm scales, it's clear that new structure and scaffolding are required. The firms measured show a steady increase in the adoption of ten key management tools, from sole practitioners (15 percent) to small boutique firms (26 percent) to medium-sized firms (44 percent).

Optimization Is the Goal

This chapter is about blueprinting your success. We draw up blueprints when we want to optimize the structure of an organization so that it operates effectively and efficiently. An optimized organization is our goal, and the 3 Rs are at the heart of such an organization:

- **Revenue:** This is the "what"; in other words, the client work.
- **Resources:** This is the "who"; in other words, the team.
- **Recipes:** This is the "how"; in other words, the processes.

These 3 Rs are what we are all managing when we try to provide value to our service organizations. We are seeking a team (our resources) that will make a commitment to deliver work (our revenue) that runs on our processes (our recipes) to provide consistent

Work is a way of bringing order to chaos, and there's a basic satisfaction in seeing that we are able to make something a little more coherent by the end of the day.

ALAIN DE BOTTON

value to our clients. (We'll talk about this in much more detail later in the book.) The organization is the container that holds it all, and it's your role as leader to design the container.

When you create an organization to add value to your target market, you are making a promise to meet the needs of that market. If you fail to live up to that promise, you let the world down in a sense: You are not the solution your clients were hoping for. I believe service organizations are beacons of hope for other entrepreneurs and business-owner clients (for that is who we serve) looking to purchase the advice and direction they need in their lives to bring order to the chaos they are navigating. We have responsibilities to the world when we bring an organization to life. As service entrepreneurs, we must take seriously the value and responsibility we hold in directing the organizations that we create.

Similar to any business, our goal in constructing our service organizations is the highest level of optimization. Optimization at its highest level creates an organization that

- provides clients with a consistent product or service every time;

- is produced by a team that follows organizational processes at the highest level of efficiency at all times; and

- results in the highest level of value provided to the client in terms of deliverables and to the organization in terms of profit.

Of course, no company operates at the highest level of optimization, but it is the organization's job to strive for and protect optimization. Anything other than that ultimately ignores the reason why the service organization exists. Yet leaders can become indifferent when they forget optimization is their purpose. Leading a growing human organization is emotional and draining, so it's easy for the entrepreneur to become lazy, disinterested, or distracted in their pursuit of optimizing their growing organization. Still, you must optimize as you grow or your organization will become sludgy, slow, and ineffective. You also have to take a break and rest so you don't become disinterested.

The goal of optimization applies to all service lines within an organization. This is a particularly difficult area of growth when your firm becomes harder to lead at the departmental stratum (13 to 25 team members). Some owners believe in service lines that are "loss leaders" yet bring in great revenue to other service lines within the organization. This is misguided. All service production comes with labor costs, which means that, while different service lines will have different profit margins, all service lines must have a profit goal. In service organizations, all our service lines relate to one another, enhance each other, and can also make other service lines difficult to fulfill. And yet, we still must have a profit goal for each service line.

As you departmentalize your organization, you must change how you track your financial statements, and you also must present your financial metrics by department (we'll discuss this further in Chapter 10). While we all want to deliver only high-profit-margin services, those are limited by demand and may depend on the foundations of other services to become available. Departmental financial tracking can show us these realities. As you saw in Dan Gertrudes's example at the beginning of this chapter, different lines of business return different margins back to the company. Still, the goal of each service line is for the price to be appropriate and the work to be produced profitably.

Stated clearly, the highest level of optimization is

- maximization of overall firm profit...

- that is a well-calculated balance of all the various services (which have varying profit margins)...

- delivered by an optimized set of resources...

- inside of an optimally built organizational structure.

This is what you are striving for, and this is what drives your firm's enterprise value (which we will discuss in Chapter 12).

The important task of the organization is to set the standard for optimization and know when that standard can be balanced with the reality of the human side of the team serving human clients. Optimization is the goal of the organization, but the employees and clients do not have to bear the weight of that goal. That resides solely with the leaders and owners. In fact, the team *serves* the organization's goal of optimization, and the clients *benefit* from that goal.

The following table shows how the optimization parameters we mentioned—the 3 Rs Framework—relate to the profit and loss components of the organization. (We've even thrown in a fourth R, results, for fun!)

The 3 Rs Framework

The Organization's Optimization Parameters	The Organization's Profit & Loss Components	The 3 Rs Framework
Consistency for the client	Revenue	Revenue
Efficiency from the team following accountable processes	Expense	Resources & Recipes
Profitability for the organization	Profit	Results

As you can see, our 3 Rs Framework is really a reflection of our profit and loss (P&L) statement, which is one of the measures of our organization's value to the world.

Consistency for the Client

Clients won't tell you this, but what they want is for you to deliver services consistently and accurately. No showboating required. Just follow your processes and deliver the same solid deliverables week after week, month after month, to produce your revenue. Call them or email them back within twenty-four hours. Do what you say you are going to do, even when you don't feel like it. You don't need rock stars or brilliant team members to do this; you just need systems and processes that smart, committed team members agree to follow. You want humans who are committed to the structure and accountability embedded in your organization that calls the team to be consistent. For service firms and agencies, being consistent is operating optimally.

CONSISTENCY

This is the ability to deliver predictable, reliable results across all aspects of the service organization—from client outcomes to team performance to operational processes and structure adoption. Consistency is not only about rigid standardization but also about balancing the need to create dependable deliverables that stakeholders can count on while caring for the team that is producing those deliverables.

As the owner, you must always seek consistency in building your organization: consistency in hiring, consistency in how you lead your team, consistency in your deliverables, consistency in how you sell, et cetera. For example, an owner who leads by doing their own calendar blocking first and overtly structuring their time makes a statement to the rest of the team that consistency matters. The opposite is arbitrary behavior that serves the owner personally. Owners who allow everyone to do what they want are committing their organization to randomness and disappointment. When each team member gets to define what they think is right, it creates chaos—the enemy of consistency. As we saw in the last chapter, it *does* matter how work gets done. Lack of clear structure and expectations has bad effects, and randomness creates variability, which makes systems less efficient. We want to optimize our firms to scale and grow, so we improve efficiency by creating consistency and minimizing randomness. Got it?

To lead consistently, partners and owners need to stay on the same page about the goal of service. Asking the team to serve in different ways depending on which owner or partner they are serving is confusing and dismantles the owners' goal of optimization. Partners may not always want exactly the same things, but it's important that they work out their differences privately, or at least have the desire to do so, for the good of the organization. It's like parenting: If a child is told two different things by two different parents on a consistent basis, that child will grow up confused and unsure of whom to please. Consistency among leaders and partners means they are not only working toward the same optimal goals but are also delivering the same message to the team.

Efficiency Following Accountable Processes

Most humans want the freedom to be inefficient. At our most belligerent, we say, "I don't want anyone telling me what to do." That was certainly my attitude when founding some of the companies I lead. It's good to recognize this reality as you ask your team to work efficiently. Inefficiency in our lives can be a place of great creation, love, and growth. As Ron Baker, author of *Implementing Value Pricing*, often quips, "Nobody wants an efficient marriage." But work is different: Inefficiency on the job wastes labor and means organizations have to use more labor than necessary to produce the same number of consistent deliverables for the client.

When service-organization entrepreneurs feel like the team is overwhelmed—the work can't get out on time or the work ends up back on the owner's plate—they often conclude that they need to hire more people. But hiring is usually a second- (or third-) order issue removed from the real problem. Efficiency is often the first-order issue to tackle. The way to do that is to dive deeper into the state of your organization's processes and how each team member is working. As we've said, unlike manufacturers that track efficiency through machine output, service-organization entrepreneurs deal with humans. Humans get distracted by their coworkers and families, forget things, get depressed, have babies, move their households across the country, and go through marriages and divorces. The owners are going through all of these things as well. And it all happens while they are trying to work "efficiently." Hiring will not create more efficient organizations, because you are only hiring more inefficient humans. Work on efficiency with your team before working on hiring more people.

You may be able to embody the goal of greater efficiency within a role. When your organization reaches a team size of 8 to 12, you can promote a technical team player to the role of project manager (or whatever you call that role). This role is meant to aid the team in knowing priorities, staying within their lanes while working, and delivering services on time. At this size of an organization, this project manager (PM) role can reduce variability and increase efficiency. With this role, when a team member struggles, they can huddle for fifteen to thirty minutes weekly with the PM to learn their role, ask questions, and get help adhering to or reordering priorities.

A project manager is a "client service" role, the area where service firms are concerned with workflow, priorities, building new and/or updated processes, and efficient work production. Project managers teach and set rhythms with your team's calendars. (We will look in depth at the word "rhythms" in Chapter 10. For now, rhythms can be defined as calendar habits that cull chaos and create more clarity.) Having your project manager lead through rhythms locks a team into the clarity of what is expected and allows it to respond with efficient service.

Profitability and Pricing

Some models of profitability have become antiquated in the professional services market. Metrics like "Revenue is broken down such that one-third of it goes to labor, one-third goes to overhead, and one-third goes to the bottom line for the owners" don't fully match the newer corporate models that modern service organizations must move toward. This kind of model works when the firm does one thing consistently over time and the founders are the main providers of the most complicated technical service delivery. But in scaling service organizations, the metrics of profitability become more complicated to track over time. The owners must always be moving toward shedding the technical work onto other people.

Initial moves toward high-level consultancy and advisory services can push a costly labor model up significantly (and thus the profit down). If this move toward advisory is managed well over time, profit can go up. In fact, profit can rise higher than what it was prior to the shift to advisory once the team members are full of work and the firm is charging higher rates for these more lucrative services. Service organizations must become more sophisticated, focusing on advisory niches, taking consulting projects, working with more complex software, and considering many other aspects that older, simpler "revenue to profit" models like the third-third-third split are less suitable for.

We made this move toward advisory a long time ago in our own firm. We didn't do it perfectly, but we would have failed if we had not relied on strategy and structure to guide us through building a labor model that supports advisory services. The markets we serve, and our teams, demand more clarity in our tracking than what older, hand-me-down metrics provided. We can no longer openly run service organizations for the obvious benefit of the owners, as they take one-third of the revenue out for themselves. If this hadn't changed, we would have struggled to attract and retain talent, since we may not have had the cash in the organization to invest in them.

Of course, profit being created solely for the owners to take was a wrong focus anyway. You can do this if you are the owner, sure, but it will limit your ability to grow. Let me give you an example I often see online: A service professional leaves their job, starts their own agency, and builds up an organization to 1 or 2 people within just a few years. They boast, "I'm making more money now than when I worked for someone just two years ago." "Yep, that's true at your size," I mumble. But when a founder of a services organization is making more money than in their last job, what you are typically seeing is that founder pulling out a disproportionate amount of revenue as their salary. They may be making six figures and still have time to travel and serve clients because there is no expensive structure to maintain in an organization with 1 to 2 people. They don't have to keep a team of 20 on expensive rotating laptops, 20 seats on a workflow product, expensive salaried senior and leadership roles (that don't all produce revenue), team care and culture gifts and retreats, and so on. When an organization is young and successful, a six-figure salary can be a setup for cutting your salary later and having to pay your leadership team more than you pay yourself. And early social-media salary "transparency" statements are hard to retract when your personal profit shrinks as you grow.

As the founder/owner, when you commit to scaling, you may have to begin prioritizing investment in the organization and in other people and putting your income lower on the priority list. I've talked earlier about having to lower my salary at a pivotal point when deciding to scale our firm. Ian has done it too. In order to grow his business from 12 to 20, from 25 to 40, and from 50 to 80, Ian had to personally invest the firm profits and his own salary back into the business to ensure his company had the right people in the right roles to grow. In fact, he invested his salary back into his company for three years (collecting no salary) to ensure they had the right count and type of resources so the organization could grow into the profits it ultimately obtained. Later, Ian hired C-suite leadership (who made more than he did) to carry on the scaling required of a larger organization. As an owner, not a hire, your responsibility and value capture are different than those of your hired leaders.

Profitability is driven when teams are supported in their growth and cared for by the organization, when there is valuable and challenging work to focus on, and when teams are invited into accountable work structures where they remain consistently productive. You can allow benchmarked metrics to drive generally what your P&L should show (e.g., fixed labor for your team should generally be around 50 percent of your revenue, give or take). But metrics

A bad system
will beat a good
person every time.

W. EDWARDS DEMING

———————————

(especially the owners' salary metric) are not meant to be an exact barometer of what your organization must attain. Instead, they are guides to help you assess where you stand in your profit reporting. (We'll touch on benchmarks, metrics, and reporting in Chapter 10.)

There are so many complexities to a service organization that every company will look different when compared to others. Components like pace of growth, maturity of growth, owners' salaries, labor costs for the team, investments in new roles, and size will all affect what your metrics will show. Greg Crabtree's book *Simple Numbers, Straight Talk, Big Profits!* should be required reading for every service-organization leader seeking to scale their company, as he dives deeply into some of these concepts, which are outside of the scope of this book.

Many service organizations want to track profit by client, but this is next to impossible to do. The goal makes sense—"Are we profitable serving this client?"—but profitability is a metric tracked for a company, not a client. As mentioned earlier and highlighted by Dan's tracking of gross margins, profitability by service line is just about as granular as you can get to track your profit. Why? Because tracking profit means tracking the revenue and the exact expense related to what you are tracking. As you departmentalize into service lines, you can also often dedicate team to those service lines; thus, you can track the revenue and labor costs of those service lines. But tracking the granularity of profit by client becomes harder because your labor costs are often not exactly identifiable to a particular client. What's more, much of the organization's resources go into expenditures that are not directly related to a single client, like technology, training, employee benefits, and toilet paper. It is hard to find a pure allocation of those resources and the amount directly attributable to each specific client.

When one of our clients wants to implement profit tracking by client, we have to ask, "Will the value of the output be greater than the effort it takes?" Sure, they can try, but it can be very cumbersome and typically requires changing their systems significantly, and then it may not turn out to be worth much. What will they do with that data? Will it change how they price clients in the future? Perhaps it will, but probably it won't. They'll have to change too much about how they do things. And meanwhile, we'll be charging them for the implementation.

Pricing your services up front collaboratively with the client leaves the opportunity for your organization to capture more of the value you are creating in your service. Unlike billing for your time, pricing takes courage as you approach your client to state boldly what your value is. Pricing your services up front in the relationship means everyone begins together on the same page. Being on the same page with your client is how profit is created in a service organization and how value is measured by the client. Team service and delivery are a large part of a service organization's ability to create consistent profit. So it makes sense that training is key to profitability. Firms that consistently provide training (at least monthly) are more valuable in the marketplace, and they have the benefit of pricing their services higher and leaving leftover profit as a result. We'll see later in the book that there is a Practice Excellence statistic showing that internal training is the leading indicator of business success.

Most seasoned entrepreneurs know that profit *is not first*—another misguided platitude. In fact, over 95 percent of the service entrepreneurs we interviewed stated that profit was a lower priority to either client satisfaction or employee engagement (or both). Profit (and loss, as it were) is the result of doing many other things right (or wrong) in leading complex scaling organizations. Service entrepreneurs will struggle to be profitable on a consistent basis when they run organizations that do any of the following (as well as many, many other examples):

- Price services out of fear or send out invoices late
- Fail to raise prices when the economy dictates they must
- Give in to being considered commodities
- Fail to leverage expertise in focused markets

- Don't have workflow systems to manage the flow of their complex knowledge deliverables

- Switch workflow software on the whim of what the owner likes best

- Struggle to create systems to hire and train teams in methodical ways

- Hold on to an underperforming team member too long

- Allow misaligned clients to stay in the firm and anchor their growth

- Make little effort to build a culture where teams feel accountable to their work

- Fail to hold their clients accountable to consume their service regularly

Of course, it makes no sense to say "Profit is first" when you are running losses. But even service entrepreneurs who do all the right things can still find themselves generating losses as they fail to pivot appropriately (and in a timely manner) in response to changing markets, recessions, economic downturns, team issues, and the necessary restructuring of their organization.

I hope you are getting it: Scaling a service organization is complex. In small firms, the owner is the strategic designer of the organization. As the firm crosses its first scaling plateau, it takes the effort of the owner and/or leadership team to make organizational design a serious part of their work. This is why, owner, you must get the work off your plate. An organization's strengths and weaknesses will be heavily influenced by the organizational design being led by the service entrepreneur. The culture of the team will also be influenced by that design and structure. Change management should become an educational part of a leader's growth as their organization grows. I'm glad you are here for this pedagogy!

4

Beyond
Good Intentions
and Plans

*Dream, design, and do. You have to design the
thing that you want to build. For us, we designed
the client journey, designed the processes for the
services we offer, and designed the organizational
structure to deliver what we want.*

STEPH HINDS
(HEAD NINJA OF GROWTHWISE;
12 EMPLOYEES)

ACK IN 2017, Ian developed an "MBA for Accountants" curriculum and ran several paying cohorts through the education, which included twenty-four lectures and twenty-four
discussion sections across the four pillars of strategy, efficiency,
growth, and management (which later became Karbon's Practice
Excellence). He developed the management curriculum with Steph
Hinds, who is one of the most notable, knowledgeable, and inspir-
ing leaders in the accounting industry. We would be remiss if we

didn't include Steph and her management advice in this book. To quote Steph, "Being an awesome leader takes work. It's not something that happens with a magic wand. It's something you need to continuously work and focus on."

Steph, as she reminded us, runs an accounting business, *not* a firm, out of lovely Newcastle, Australia. With her business partner, Alan Spicer, Steph started Growthwise almost sixteen years ago (at time of writing). Her journey can be broken down into three different five-year journeys. She explained:

> When designing your business, you need to question every-thing—every role and every task—and literally get them out on the whiteboard and piece them back together in a way that works for the business you're trying to build.

In her first five years, she, like most people, was chasing revenue growth. In her next five years, it was profit. And now (and for the foreseeable future) it is a dollar-value profit baseline to enable Alan and her to retire sometime in the future. When they make more than that, they plow the money back into the business:

> Over time, I've started to understand what business was about. I've tested lots of things over the years. Some stuff has worked, and some stuff hasn't. However, the success of a business is always highly reliant on brilliant leadership.

But the path wasn't just a simple straight line. Going through their second five-year journey, Growthwise grew to 17 people, and Steph recalls that at about 15 employees, they hit the scaling plateau:

> We did a terrible thing back then, growing to 17 people with a flat structure. It was horrendously bad. The reality is that we couldn't deal with more than 15 people in our current structure.

Since then, Steph, as an exemplar of what we discussed in Chapter 1, has understood what it means to be an entrepreneurial leader of a professional services business. She knows what she wants, and she knows what she and her business partner want with the business overall:

I don't want to be the biggest accounting business in Australia. What we care about is doing fun work, and, for me, that is getting to spend time directly with clients to help them out. Our dream is that our staff will take over the business and make it their own, and continue the relationships with our clients to take them to the end of their business life. That is literally our ultimate dream.

The Theory—and Practice—of Evolution

Ian Vacin

Like people, organizations shift and evolve over time. Each person you add changes the culture (hopefully for the better), adds more organizational weight, and adds more to manage for the founder/owners. As discussed in the last chapter, the organization encounters significant changes as it scales and must adapt by adding processes and complex structures (strata) like management, departments, and leadership layers. All this comes at a cost, which, if not managed and balanced correctly, leads to corporate sludge, culture clashes, and lower revenue per employee (among other things). As a leader, you need to know when to add these structures while optimizing for the firm in terms of its culture and profitability. But why do these strata exist, and how do we know when to take action to add more complexity so that an organization can scale?

In the process of writing this book, Jason and I met with over a hundred progressive entrepreneurial owners to understand in depth their journeys, fears, failures, successes, and stories. Those interviews reminded us of the thousands upon thousands of service firm owners we have met at events and conferences through the years looking for advice, reassurance, and best practices on how to grow and scale their firms. What is interesting is that even those firm owners who are viewed as successful have the same questions you might have when reading this book—questions like these:

- When should I hire the next person?

- Based on my firm's size, what roles should I keep or add to be most effective?

- Am I ready for a manager or senior leader?

- When do I need to add another layer of management or an additional department?

- What will it cost, and how will that team addition impact my firm's profitability?

- Is my firm organized correctly? Does it need to change, and if so, how?

- What firm structures exist, and when should I shift my organizational design?

- Can we handle the change-management messaging for this change to be successful?

- Why do I feel like I don't understand what is happening like I did in years past?

- Am I making the right decisions?

- Why do I feel like my head is spinning?

Let's take a deep breath. As founder/owners, we *all* have those thoughts in our heads. It is what drives us to achieve new heights, and those same thoughts identify when we need to make a change because we sense something isn't right within our organization. They lead us to seek answers. So let's look together at the components (teams and roles) of an organization so you can understand how to design the best organization to perform optimally for what you want.

The Constraints of Teams

Over the years, I have had the pleasure of working with and leading teams at companies in various business stages of growth, from start-ups (MetaEdge) to scaleups (Tefen, Netigy, Karbon) to enterprises (BEA Systems, Xero, Intuit, PwC), as well as to advise and consult with numerous startups and scaleups. While each business looked different, the fundamental constraints of the teams looked the same. Large teams felt disconnected and inefficient, while smaller teams felt overstretched and more variable. When running large teams, I always felt I was in perpetual one-on-ones with no time to do actual work. When managing small teams, I felt like I knew where things were at but that we just couldn't keep up with the demands of the business. And the question always loomed in my head: What is the ideal manager-to-staff ratio that would optimize everything—visibility, control, individual ownership, productivity, accountability, and profitability?

That is why, years ago, I adopted the practice of asking owners three basic questions to quickly understand their firms:

- Resources: How large (in full-time equivalents) is your firm?

- Revenue: What are your various service lines, and what is your client count?

- Structure: How are you structured? (Does everyone do everything, or are you departmentalized?)

From these questions, I can easily estimate how the firm operates and visualize their strata. For service organizations (and specifically for accounting firms), I can quickly determine their owner-to-employee ratio, manager-to-employee ratio, number of departments, headcount per department, and whether it is efficient or inefficient. How can I do this? Simple: team dynamics.

Have you ever been on a high-performing team? What were the characteristics of the manager, captain, or leader of the team?

How was it working with others on the team? High trust? Engaging work? Was there personal ownership and accountability of the work in your control? It felt great, didn't it? That team delivered what they wanted and could take on anything. We want to emulate that for our own teams.

Now think of the size of the team. Typically, those teams are not too small and not too large—they are in the Goldilocks zone. When I worked at Intuit, the then-CEO, Brad Smith, would always say that the highest-performing teams were "two-pizza teams." This translated to somewhere between 6 and 8 people, depending on the pizza sizes and the hunger of the team members. The best-performing teams are manageable, purpose-driven, and diverse and have highly engaged team members. So how big should your firm be, and how big should your various teams or departments be?

On the way to answering the question about firm size, let's look at three broad staff levels in service organizations: owners/partners, managers, and individual contributors (IC)—in other words, those who do the work (IC), those who manage the work (managers), and those who manage the firm (owners and/or partners). After we asked hundreds of service firms, it was evident that the average firm would be somewhere around a 1:12 owner/partner-to-IC ratio and 1:8 manager-to-IC ratio. Later, using large quantitative surveys at Intuit, Xero, and Karbon (plus our Practice Excellence survey), I was able to validate these anecdotal averages.

MANAGEMENT RATIO

This is the ratio of leaders (or managers) to the team members who report to them. The ratio is limited by the complexity of the work, the ability of the team members within the pod, and the time needed to communicate and review work on a consistent basis.

You say that this doesn't match your firm or those of your colleagues? It might not. In fact, in our survey for the book, the results showed that accounting firms on average hired their first manager at 6 employees and created their first department at 9 employees (this is lower than the averages we saw from the long-term broader studies). Those averages quoted above are based on a normal distribution that ranges widely for owner/partner-to-IC ratios (from 1 to 25) and for manager-to-IC ratios (from 4 to 12). The industry you are in, the clients you serve, and even the service lines you offer can all adjust your firm's ideal ratios from the norm. However, the average provides us with guidance on where the majority of firm owners have consciously decided to add management layers to enable a firm to successfully operate.

Interestingly enough, when we analyzed the data on our Practice Excellence survey results, step-change differences emerged (defined by Practice Excellence score and revenue per employee). A step-change in data analysis refers to when values abruptly move from one stable state to another, often appearing as a distinct "step" when represented on a graph. What can be seen in the data is that less successful firms appeared at key employee sizes (e.g., 8 to 12 employees), while more successful firms appeared at other sizes (e.g., 20 to 30 employees). When we evaluated this further, the step-changes we observed not only overlapped where successful firms had optimized team dynamics but also indicated where lower-performing firms were struggling with scaling plateaus and how to manage a team.

These observations reinforce the concept and factors of span of control (SOC)—our first major component of teams. SOC refers to the number of people reporting to a given manager. While the average might be 1:8 manager-to-ICs, your ideal number might be lower (narrower SOC) or higher (wider SOC), depending on a number of factors, including the following:

- Manager engagement: Do you want them more or less engaged with the team? Are they seasoned managers or new to management?

- Manager responsibilities: Are they managing 100 percent of their time, or are they also producing work and working with clients?

- Work type: Consulting and advisory jobs are different from copywriting or bookkeeping jobs. If the work is less technical, then a wider SOC may be possible.

- Industry: Accounting, design, engineering, and consultancies all have varying levels of complexity to their work. Thus, they can have wider or narrower SOCs, as the needs of managers and technical experts change depending on the type of work being done.

- Organization structure: This is defined by orientation, departmentalization, talent level, and variation. Flat structures have wide SOCs by design.

The simple observation around team dynamics becomes very important in our organizational design. It helps us understand how to set the various strata for management, departments, and leadership using our own internal optimal team sizes to ensure a high-performing organization that maximizes our revenue per employee, rather than being a drag on it.

The Separation of Roles

A second component of teams is oversight. Some teams have managers at the helm, while others have leaders. The roles have various titles, such as "lead," "senior," "manager," and "director." All these variations depend on the size of the organization, the requirements for the team, and where the team sits within the organizational structure. Whatever their title, it's critical to note that these oversight roles must operate as a proxy of the founder/owner. This means that when the senior team member is leading a team without the owners present, they are a proxy of the owner and acting on their behalf. You want the senior leaders to lead *as if* you, the owner, were leading. We don't build leadership teams so they can do whatever they want—all leaders consistently lead with the same values and vision that the founder/owners espouse.

When you are a one-person band, you, as the founder/owner, wear all three hats—doer (IC), manager, and leader. But as you grow, the manager role emerges, and then later the leadership role emerges—hence the strata that we defined in the previous chapter. Again, team dynamics are at play here, dictating when we should add the next management person to our overhead.

As the firm grows, these roles of ICs, managers, and leaders become more defined and more stratified. Firms scaling through the departmental and leadership strata (more than 12 employees) will see these roles and responsibilities being fully defined. This separation of roles is an important component as we think about how our organizational design needs to evolve as our firm grows. We've provided a quick-reference chart to give you some perspective on the differences between the three role types.

Roles and Responsibilities:
Key Questions Each Role Should Be Asking

	Doers	Managers	Leadership
First Thing	What has changed with my projects/ clients since I last checked?	What has changed across the team since I last checked?	What is happening across the firm?
Urgency	Are there any urgent issues with my clients?	Are we on track to hit our deadlines and meet our goals?	Are our clients happy?
Prioritization	What are my priorities? Have they shifted?	Are we servicing our clients? Are our processes sufficient?	Do we have the resources and tools we need to be successful?
Projects	Are my projects coming along as expected?	How can we do things more efficiently as a team?	How do we drive more business from new or existing clients?
Looking Ahead	Will I meet my deadlines? On time? At quality?	What cross-sell or up-sell opportunities exist?	Are we profitable? What should we change or double down on?
Vantage Point	My	Our	Us

Roles and Responsibilities:
Accountability, Visibility, and Transparency

	Doers	Managers	Leadership
Ownership	Own my clients and projects	Own the outcomes of the team	Own the outcomes of the firm
Operating Mechanisms	Provide weekly updates on where projects stand	Establish and maintain team operating mechanisms	Monitor customer satisfaction, profitability, and capacity
Communication	Speak up on what has been learned and what is needed	Support and champion the needs of the team	Listen to the team and expeditiously remove barriers
Role	Champion the needs of the client	Foster an environment of sharing	Ensure a positive work environment

With that said, managers and leaders are two different things and are needed at very different times and sizes of firm. Leaders need more freedom to operate, while managers need more direction and guidance (not to mention the cost difference between the two types of resources). Think back to the high-performing teams you have worked in and the characteristics of those managers. Now, think about the amazing companies you have been a part of and the characteristics of their leaders. As a founder/owner of a small firm, you may need to emulate *both* the leader and manager at this moment in time. If your firm is (or will become) larger, you need to be the best leader you can be and rely on your managers to represent you appropriately to the team when helping them get the work done.

To paint a clearer picture, remember that a leader and a manager act very differently:

Leader Versus Manager

Persuades and influences vs.
Dictates and directs

Establishes strategic vision vs.
Handles tactical execution

Embraces calculated uncertainty vs.
Seeks predictable outcomes

Empowers and develops talent vs.
Oversees and assigns tasks

Imagines future possibilities vs.
Achieves current targets

Pioneers innovative pathways vs.
Optimizes existing systems

Builds loyalty through purpose vs.
Maintains order through authority

What Type of Leader Are You?

Now, let's talk about you, the founder/owner, and your role. Are you a leader, an entrepreneur, or an entrepreneurial leader? These are not the same and will dictate if you need to bring a leader into your organization sooner rather than later. But what are the differences?

As we've just seen, the difference between leaders and managers is that leaders are able to influence and motivate others to contribute to the organization's success, while managers will drive and control a team to achieve a specific provided objective (often as a proxy of the leader). The difference between leaders and entrepreneurs is that leaders guide an organization toward success, while entrepreneurs start, create, and build a successful business. As such, entrepreneurs can drive an organization to initial success, and leaders can drive an organization to additional levels of success (hopefully repeatedly). In comparison to a leader and an entrepreneur, an entrepreneurial leader is unique in that they are driven, purposeful, empowering, risk-taking, innovative, visionary, resourceful, resilient, impatient, and unsatisfied. Simply stated, an entrepreneurial leader combines the innovative spirit and vision of an entrepreneur with the ability to influence and motivate others to lead an organization.

For growing organizations, entrepreneurial leaders are extremely valuable, as they not only have the broad set of skills necessary to foresee the scaling plateaus but can also leverage their innovative, problem-solving skills to intentionally overcome them. Organizations with no entrepreneurial leaders find it difficult to overcome the scaling plateaus, as the founder/owner relies on their perseverance and stubbornness to try various approaches to succeed and typically attacks the issue too late, once the team is already struggling, further complicating the situation. If you are in a situation where you don't have an entrepreneurial leader on the team, you need to create a close partnership between the founder/owner and the leaders of the organization. Then, ensure the collective leadership team takes the necessary time each quarter (or semi-annually) to evaluate the landscape and proactively put plans in place to overcome the landmines facing the organization in the near and distant future.

As Jason and I are founder/owners ourselves, we can't stress enough that you need self-awareness of your own capabilities and shortcomings. Just because you founded the business doesn't mean you should lead it to new levels of success or frontiers. In most cases, founders need to learn how to support the firm's future stages of growth. This was the case for Jason, as he's already described, and it involved tough moments, hard conversations, and deep soul searching. In other cases, a founder needs to take a step back and let others lead the organization to new levels of success. That was the case for me personally.

After co-leading Karbon (from inception to 150 people), I found that we needed a new, different group of leaders. I had learned how to lead through its first phase of founder-led growth by being successful as a generalist (knowing a little bit of everything), but now we needed to hire, manage, and lead departments of specialists. Could I do it? Sure. But was I the best person to lead it? Probably not. After I stepped back, we quickly went from 40 percent to greater than 50 percent year-over-year growth as a business. This wasn't an easy decision, but it was the right decision. The best thing for the business was for me to step back, hand over the reins, and then coach and mentor the other leaders, while driving a subsection of the business.

In the long term, the organization will be successful due to the collective people involved, and not because of the efforts of the founder/owners or the heroics of the early few. You need to find, in time, the managers and leaders that you, the founder/owner, can put on your shoulders to lead your organization to new heights. Entrepreneurship is a humbling experience, so don't let your ego hold the organization back.

Interested in learning what type of leader you are? Take the assessment at the book's website.

Types of Service Organizations

Now let's look at how an organization evolves to overcome its first scaling plateau, with a lens on how its organizational design evolves over time.

Typically, at first, it is just the founder/owner who is a technician in the firm's service line(s). As the client base is established, the founder/owner grows the team with additional employees who either are technicians or can help by removing the load of lower-level activities, such as administrative work. As the firm continues to grow, that method of growth is further pursued because (a) it is working and (b) it is familiar. As soon as the boundaries of team dynamics are reached for that firm/team, the first scaling plateau starts to be felt. Consciously or not, the team reacts by gravitating to more formalized roles between the team members to absorb the management requirements that need to be fulfilled. Are they operating optimally? Probably not. They are now collectively struggling to keep above the water line in terms of managing their work and clients.

At this stage, we typically hear a founder/owner say that the organization doesn't feel right to them. They describe the moment as follows:

- "I don't feel like I know what everyone is doing."

- "I am worried about losing my best employees—they appear to be overwhelmed."

- "I don't feel like I am a successful leader. We aren't meeting the goals we set."

- "I feel like I am starting from the beginning and relearning as we go."

At this first scaling plateau, typically between 8 and 20 employees, it isn't about adding leadership, but rather about adding management. The founder/owner is still the client-facing and internal leader, but they struggle to keep everything operationally efficient and organized while managing their own client work. So at this stage, it is time to promote (or add) some managers to the team.

Before this plateau, the firm is usually a team of generalists that can do anything and everything for a client. Each generalist typically owns a client holistically, doing almost everything that is needed for the client. The specialization is typically not along service lines, but rather according to industry or client vertical specialization. Perhaps one team member is focused on a given general client category, firm revenue size, or industry vertical. This structure hits a very hard scaling plateau between 8 and 12 people as it becomes hard to find additional people with this "can do everything" skill set, more costly to hire these additionally needed resources (than more focused, junior team members), and extremely difficult to manage overall due to the size of the team. A founder/owner will communicate to others that they feel like "the organization has slowed down." This is a sign that there is a lack of communication, attention, and oversight over the team caused by its increased size, with no additional management added.

At this stage, the firm starts to embody a hybrid organizational design that is a mixture of vertically oriented (a flat structure where everyone does everything for a client) and horizontally oriented (a hierarchical structure that is departmentalized). This is where the organization begins to build the strata of management and departments in an effort to handle the negative effects of overstretched team dynamics.

Whether it is an accounting firm adding a tax or advisory department or a design agency adding full-service brand management and high-level strategy offerings, the hybrid organization begins to departmentalize the technical expertise of the founder/owner (or other high-value services) that requires specialized resources. The firm might also group its low-value services (e.g., bookkeeping for a full-service accounting firm, or social media management for a marketing agency) into a department to create its first "center of excellence," with the goal of staffing it with more junior team members to create cost and efficiency advantages.

At this hybrid-organization point, there is at least one additional department that is separated from the original central operations of the firm. This effort right-sizes the manager-to-IC ratio, enabling the firm to grow into the newly formed department(s). This singular step of organizational design evolution is, from our extensive research, a major catalyst for overcoming the first scaling plateau, enabling the firm to grow from a bloated single-team structure (up to 12 people) to a two-team structure with room to grow to up to 25 people. Design changes like this also open up the capacity abilities of more focused teams to produce more revenue in an efficient way.

From this point, the firm begins to develop departments (or pods) where economies of scale are pursued for main service lines driving firm efficiency and increased clients per employee, and subsequently higher revenue per employee. In our examples of an accounting firm and a design agency, a full-service accounting firm might expand to have dedicated departments for accounting/ bookkeeping, tax, advisory, and more. Likewise, a design agency might evolve to have dedicated departments for creative, client services, and production. This pursuit to create departments or pods transforms the organization from a hybrid design to a horizontal (hierarchical, stratified) structure. It is this hierarchical structure that the firm will maintain as it continues to grow.

POD

A dedicated team focused on delivering services to a given set of clients, or, more typically, providing a particular set of service deliverables for the firm's overall client base. A pod typically has a multidisciplinary team all formed closely together to make service more efficient, as the pod is most familiar with the clients they serve.

As the firm grows past the 25-to-30-employee stage, the organization builds its leadership stratum. This helps the service organization move from a traditional owner/partner model to operating like a proper business with a proper structure that includes not only the production departments but all the other areas, like sales and marketing, R&D, finance, HR, legal, administrative, and executive functions. Previously, leadership roles were reserved for elevated operational roles or partnership-like additions, but now C-suite roles start to be added over time. New business positions will be added, such as these:

- CEO: Lead, provide vision, and implement the founder/owner plan

- Operations manager: Ensure every process runs smoothly

- Business development manager: Seek new clients

- Service delivery expert: Provide specialized services to a niche audience

- Client manager: Ensure all clients start on the right foot

- IT specialist: Manage technology for the team and clients

Now, organizations do not always evolve and change just as we've described. Perhaps your firm is 16 people today and you have already moved into a hierarchical, stratified structure with two functional departments. That's great, and it will help you reduce the burden of the scaling plateau that you'll face from 8 to 20 employees. The journey of restructuring we've taken you through is intended to provide you with insights into the typical *forced* transition that firms experience as team dynamics and organizational constraints require them to evolve from a vertical-oriented (flat) to a horizontal-oriented (hierarchical) structure. It also gives you a roadmap for thinking strategically about how to evolve your firm and its structures over time to make the right hires at the right time, so you can successfully navigate the difficulties firms face at these various scaling plateaus.

Business Versus Agency/Practice

For service businesses, one of the most classic scaling issues is running your firm like an "agency" or "practice" rather than a business. Do you recall what Steph said at the beginning of the chapter? She emphasized that she ran a "business," not a "firm." You need to do the same.

If you want to grow and scale your business so it can be a team of 40, 50, or larger, it has to transition from a partnership model to a C-suite business structure. Once you have more than two partners, you ultimately have too many "cooks in the kitchen." Fiefdoms form, political agendas can get set, motivations diverge, and the organization begins to slow down. In our Practice Excellence survey results, this was clearly present at medium-sized firms (50 to

100 employees), which exhibited an overall 7 percent decrease in their Practice Excellence score. This decrease shows that firms experience corporate sludge and an inefficient use of resources. If this situation applies to your organization, you must address it head-on as you go through additional organization restructurings.

The concepts in this chapter provide context and color for why firms struggle to scale and grow, plus the recipes for success. When you start your firm, your strategy is most important. When you scale your firm, your organizational design and structures become most important, to enable you to scaffold and grow. You need to evolve your firm into a proper business, and you need to do it thoughtfully and intentionally. Each organization has its own set of team dynamics and optimal sizes (although still closely aligned to the ratios mentioned earlier), and the profitability of your organization is directly related to the existence of fully staffed operational departments or pods. You need to be mindful of when to add new business functions and departments that support client growth, as well as when to add people management to create a high-performing organization. We'll explore in the next few chapters how to manage our revenue and capacity to ensure our organization is effective, efficient, and properly resourced.

Okay, Now What?

We've looked at the situation and the realities. We've given you a sense of the kinds of things you're going to need to do to scale your company sensibly. When the rubber hits the road, we'll show you how to do what you're going to have to do. Right now, as we're about to cross that bridge, here are some of the questions we expect you're carrying in your mind:

- Are there beliefs and actions I need to change about my leadership that would support my organization's growth, instead of hindering it?

- Do I want "what it means" to scale my services firm?

- Do I align with any of the stories of service entrepreneurs that have helped me to see the flaws in my own organizational design?

- Have I prioritized my own desire for personal profit, rather than allowed my organization to have what it needs to grow and thrive?

- Do I have the right organizational structure to grow, or is it now clear that I must change our structure to continue to scale?

- Do I need more courage to do what is right to grow my service organization, as opposed to being distracted, disinterested, or feeling defeated by the work of scaling?

- Is there anyone I need to promote, fire, or hire? What is my next team move?

- Is my organization at a scaling plateau that I need to push through?

Let's start answering those questions.

PART II

CAPACITY

&

PLANNING

5

Revenue First, Everything Else Second

Our approach is to give a lot of autonomy and delegate decision making down into the organization. We want to reduce silos, keep things very lean and flat. As such, our directors manage most client relationships and have ownership to define or revise engagement scope, pricing, and deadlines.

MOEZ BAWANIA, CPA, CA
(CO-FOUNDER OF AMLB; 19 EMPLOYEES)

STARTING IN late 2019 and through the heart of COVID-19, Moez and his business partner, Ally Ladha, both first-generation immigrant families in Canada, built an amazing virtual finance and CFO advisory business serving all of Canada. Though the early years were tough, it gave them the experience and grit that has propelled their business to grow 40 percent year over year. Today, their global team of 19 professionals serves a portfolio of over sixty-five entrepreneurial and nonprofit organizations. Because a primary service line is CFO advisory, they know a lot about giving advice on pricing, interpreting financials, and the importance of revenue, costs, and profit. Moez says:

> Over time, we have been able to enable our cloud accountants to do most of the CFO advisory work with our clients. In general, we tell the team that 70 percent of your time should be on client work, 15 percent on training and development plus coaching, and another 15 percent on admin, vacations, or whatever else you have.

Fans of Warren Buffett, Moez and Ally are extremely thoughtful about how to build the business and leverage their understanding of their revenue to guide their business decisions on staffing, planning, and workflow efficiency. They spend time looking at their revenue and client makeup and work hard to ensure they drive a diversified portfolio of clients to minimize the risks of having too many large clients with disproportional weight on their revenue and future. In addition, they use their forecasted revenue to set their quarterly capacity planning and short-term load balancing (a concept we'll address later). Over time, through trial and error, they have been able to pinpoint the amount of revenue each of their employees can manage, to drive ultimate efficiency:

> The way we forecast capacity is based on revenue serviced. We use a custom-built pricing model during our sales process to set prices and internally to establish "budgeted revenue per role." The budgeted revenue is based on estimated hours multiplied by hourly rates and takes into account a number of variables, such as the nature and frequency of services to be provided, and allows for adjustments. And then for every cloud accountant on the team, we provide an "annual revenue serviced" target. By doing this, we simplify the equation: We ensure our staff aren't overloaded and everyone is focused on client service quality rather than quantity, while the business grows in a sustainable manner by delivering on revenue and gross and net margin targets.

Planning Future Revenue

Jason Blumer

In Part Two, Ian and I are going down deep into the company and working on the building blocks of a service organization. We'll focus more practically on determining human capacity. We said at the beginning of the book that we will prove that if you are struggling in any way with the growth of your service organization, the answer will be to design your organization better. Now let's put legs to that claim and use this chapter to determine your service organization's human capacity. Then we'll help you design your better org.

All human capacity is not the same. Stated another way, all capacity in your organization is not of the same value. Think about your organization. Do you pay everyone the same salary? Why does your technical expert make more than your office administrator? When you interviewed a manager for one of your departments, did they ask for more money than you were offering, and did you end up agreeing to a higher salary? The money we pay for human capacity represents the perception of value of that pay.

If people aren't paid the same, then we can assume that their capacity is not of the same value. As an intentional leader, you get to decide which capacity to use on the type of revenue you are seeking to fulfill. A point we have not made yet is that the revenue you decide to take into your organization has everything to do with determining how much human capacity you have, need, should add, or need to get rid of. The fact that a service organization, like a firm, agency, or consultancy, has revenue is the very justification for having capacity available to service that revenue in the first place.

HUMAN CAPACITY

The amount of time and effort a person can provide over a given period, taking into account their physical, mental, and emotional states. While machine capacity is typically consistent week over week, human capacity will be variable due to the complexities of each employee's life.

A common question for people who are growing service orgs is, "Do I hire before I have the revenue and then go get revenue, or do I wait until I have revenue and then go hire?" Theoretically, the answer is easy. The only reason you need capacity is because you have revenue in the first place. If you had zero revenue in your organization, then you would need zero capacity. Determining capacity always has to do with your revenue first. So, in theory, you shouldn't increase your capacity availability by hiring until you have the revenue to justify it. Simple!

But it's not that simple, is it? Sometimes we take a risk that the revenue is coming in the future so we'll have the right person in place when we need them. The point is: Revenue—either current or anticipated—is the reason we need to manage capacity. To manage your team's capacity, you need to know a lot of things about your revenue... things that are hard to know.

Here are seven revenue considerations that affect how you connect your revenue to your team's capacity:

Volume: How much revenue will I get next month? Next quarter? Next year?

Timing: What time of year will the revenue come in? How quickly?

Complexity: Will the revenue be easy to service, or is the scope complex?

Cadence: Does your revenue have a beginning and end point to the deliverable (project-based), or is your revenue ongoing (recurring)?

Novelty: Does the revenue have aspects to it that are new or unknown to those trying to service it?

Placement: Does the revenue have to be serviced by the owner and leaders, or can those without leadership responsibilities service it (i.e., strategic versus tactical)?

Probability: Is your revenue guaranteed (contracted), contingent (performance-based), or planned (demand forecasted)?

You may feel like the revenue that is coming into your service organization is something you lack control over as the founder/owner/leader. You would be wrong. Other industries, like mature product and SAAS companies (like Ian's company Karbon), use metrics like monthly recurring revenue, customer lifetime value, annual recurring revenue/FTE, and other revenue forecasting metrics to understand their performance, identify trends, and make informed decisions about pricing, resource allocation, and market positioning. Service organizations must do this too, especially as they grow larger and more complex.

At a certain point, I realized our firm's revenue risk was very high. If we lost one client paying $12,000 per month, it would blow a big hole in our income for the month because the replacement of that kind of revenue has a very long sales cycle. Similarly, if we lost a senior member of our team that was serving our more specialized and complex revenue, it would be hard to replace them. So we decided to de-risk our portfolio: broaden our revenue mix, move down the value chain, and even consider smaller acquisitions to move our firm model faster. It left us with a less risky model of revenue production to support. This is an example of how, as the owner, planning your revenue is fully in your hands and is something strategic service-organization owners commit themselves to so they can determine their human capacity accurately.

The Power of Recurring Revenue

If your revenue has a predictable cadence, where it comes in at a fixed price each week, month, or quarter, then you can track your monthly recurring revenue (MRR). This is a number we watch in our own firm like a hawk. It's the total bucket of cash flow coming in and can be compared to your average operating expenditures to see if you track above or below your operating expenses. Because you are reviewing MRR and average monthly operating expenditures, you have a consistent and predictable mechanism for understanding the financial health of the firm. If some of your revenue comes in annually, monthly, quarterly, or at other times, then you may take your average annual revenue for all clients and divide by twelve to get to your MRR. Now take your MRR and divide that by your number of clients to arrive at your average revenue per client/customer (ARPC). (We'll explore more metrics later in Chapter 10.) This is also a number that gives you a sense of what type of revenue you are bringing in as you grow. When our firm had to de-risk our revenue, we were working to bring our ARPC down considerably so that our revenue risk was spread more evenly across more clients with less monthly revenue.

RECURRING REVENUE

The value of recurring revenue is in its predictability, which is why we seek to turn revenue into a recurrence. The contract generally stipulates a fixed price the client agrees to pay on the recurrence. Recurring revenue is generally contracted over a long period (e.g., six to twelve to eighteen months) and allows for the ability to match pricing to services. That is, if you draft your recurring price weekly (as can be done with CFO engagements), that can easily be matched up to the value being delivered weekly.

Sometimes you want to sell less revenue when you don't have the capacity you need to fulfill more revenue. In those times, you are balancing the revenue coming in with the capacity you have available to service it. You can do this by offering the client a later start date to the recurring contract. In fact, you can't just sell any revenue you want. You have to bring in the type of revenue that can continually be serviced more and more by your team (and less and less by the owner/leaders). Founders who carry the sales role in the organization will often sell the type of revenue *they* enjoy fulfilling, or even revenue that only they can fulfill. You need to stop and ask yourself, "Can my team service this revenue, or will I have to service it?" Getting the mix wrong can really slow a firm's growth and be the reason you hit your first scaling plateau.

Concurrent Versus Future Capacity

In addition to knowing your revenue, MRR, ARPC, and other metrics, it's also important to note that determining human capacity has everything to do with planning for the future. If you are currently servicing revenue with the human capacity you have now (in the present), then you have already made your determinations about capacity, whether you've done that well or poorly. The deliverables your team is working on today are not a planning function, but rather an operational/efficiency function of your organization. Work today is all about being as consistent, efficient, and excellent as possible with the revenue you already have. We'll call this focus on the present *concurrent* capacity usage. This is an important point, because if you are struggling to fulfill your revenue requirements in the present, then it is hard to solve by hiring new team members. Why? Because, like capacity planning, hiring also has to do with planning and anticipating revenue in the future.

Essentially, hiring for the future happens when you anticipate future revenue growth. Hiring has a long lead time, since you need to get new team members onboarded and up to speed to solve any issues with the lack of current capacity. If you wait until you have the revenue, you won't have the person in place soon enough to service it. Also, your capacity will be temporarily diminished by the time and effort required to hire someone and get them up to speed. From our survey, the average firm takes 2.4 months to hire someone and another 5 months to have that person be onboarded, trained, and accretive. In our advisory firm, we expect a new team member to be completely onboarded after ninety days and then to be on their own in their role after six months. Knowing our lead time is six months, we can't just expect a new team member to jump in and be a real powerhouse in serving the capacity needs of clients *concurrently*. We must give them time to onboard, and thus we anticipate they will be serving future revenue, not current revenue. Make sense?

It might look like this:

Resources	Revenue
Who: The team	What: The client work
Concurrent capacity (trained and fully onboarded team)...	... serves current clients (clients already scoped and contracted).
Hiring (a future activity that will require the team to train to get up to speed) for capacity to...	... serve revenue planning in the future (clients not yet onboarded but anticipated).

Another complexity of hiring and onboarding a new team member is that it will necessarily lead to a reduction in other team members' output, since current team members will have to support the new hire as they get up to speed. This reduction in capacity will probably happen in your senior and manager levels, since those levels are created to support the onboarding of new teams and team members. To level up your sophistication in capacity management, your service organization will be successful when you make planning the revenue you take or allow in the future a part of learning and documenting the basis of your team's capacity. What we mean is that your resources and revenue planning always go together in a scaling service organization, as shown in the table. Don't allow these to be divorced from one another.

Stated another way, you solve capacity issues in the future, not in the present. If you do have capacity planning complexities in the present, they are solved through project management, work prioritization, and load balancing (a topic we'll address in Chapter 11) with the knowledge that you *will* miss deadlines, provide lower-quality work, or work overtime if you don't manage them intentionally. One way we manage this is to put into a senior team member's role a "capacity bridge" component. That is, for ninety days their role as a senior team member is to be a capacity bridge for the new team member, who is meant to service concurrent revenue. The senior team member will walk alongside the new one as they get up to speed in service. The capacity-bridge component in the senior role can also be applied when we lose team members—the "bridge" team member can step in and fulfill concurrent revenue while we hire and get a new team member up to speed. This is a team design that can save your bacon when revenue unexpectedly leaves or dumps into your firm.

Naturally, while a senior team member who has a bridge component in their role can really save your client service during disruptive times, this aspect of their role can also take some of their capacity away for servicing revenue. Managing all of this can get complex. These are conscious concurrent business decisions to make the most of a potential future planning imbalance. Wise leaders look ahead to see what revenue is coming, manage their concurrent capacity balances, and plan their capacity accordingly *in the future*, depending on the team they have or will hire then.

So, to state it again: First, plan your revenue in the future, *then* determine your human capacity needs.

Revenue planning is an owner or leader's role and is highly strategic. On the other hand, concurrent revenue fulfillment (not planning) is an operational function and can reside in project management, operations, and senior technical roles. Strategic activities sit in the top part of the team chart (i.e., the org or accountability chart), while efficiency and operational work and decisions sit in the technical leadership parts of your team chart. In the design of the organization, revenue fulfillment roles are meant to move efficiently and not be bogged down with the friction of strategy and selling. Planning roles have high friction in them and thus need to be at a level where they do not slow down revenue fulfillment. Make sure the right roles in your organization are performing these appropriate functions. In our survey of firm owners, only 48 percent complete at least quarterly revenue planning, with 34 percent saying they don't conduct revenue planning at all or only do it ad hoc.

Here are the seven revenue planning considerations again, but with related human capacity planning considerations:

Volume: A large amount of revenue produces the need for large amounts of capacity. So larger teams make large volumes of revenue intake possible. As the team remains large, remember that your need for a high volume of revenue remains high too. As the team reaches a certain girth, this leads organizations to add more sophisticated RevOps and BizDev departments to bring revenue in more quickly and predictably.

Timing: If revenue begins to accelerate or slow down, in time that will overuse or underuse capacity, so consider pushing clients to different start dates to better match your capacity availability. This is fully within your power and a great strategic lever to pull. Higher speeds of revenue coming in may create the need for a traffic manager role (usually in large service organizations) who maintains the context of all revenue and can aid leaders in making quick capacity-placement decisions.

Complexity: Since all revenue in service organizations is defined by scope, multiple layers of scope can overcomplicate the capacity needs of the organization. Complex scope also causes friction and increases learning curves, thus making revenue production less effi-cient. Consider lowering the complexity of what you sell when you have low capacity or only junior team members on your capacity bench.

Cadence: Recurring revenue is predictable, so service-organization leaders like it. But if your human capacity is not buttoned up, you may need to turn recurring revenue into an initial project, if possi-ble, while you get ready for the recurring cadence to come in more permanently. The ICs (doers) on your team can efficiently produce recurring revenue profitably, while the senior or manager levels may have to produce the discovery or project deliverables.

Novelty: Services that are generally new or unknown to the team (or reflect new services that you have created) use more capacity in the research/understanding phase. Since new services can be less profitable, owner/leaders should be careful about getting too much novel revenue if the capacity is tight and the firm doesn't have room for learning and research. Newly created services are great ways to create revenue, but you may have to bridge that revenue through a senior role (or even the owner) that can train other team members to perform the work. As a note, when you sell services that are attached to implementing or supporting a new piece of software (i.e., new to your team), that falls into the "novelty" category of revenue fulfillment.

Placement: Owners can become overwhelmed if they keep sell-ing revenue that can be fulfilled only by them (as we mentioned earlier). Consider the roles you intend to place the sold revenue into so that you can match the revenue situation with your current human-capacity reality. Place simple recurring revenue with junior team members and reserve the senior capacity for more complex revenue. We are emphasizing that you can't just place revenue ful-fillment wherever you want—it must be placed with the right team so that revenue is produced as efficiently as possible.

Probability: Future revenue isn't a guarantee. Outside events can shorten or even cancel promised revenue. Apply a probability percentage to each revenue stream and ensure you mathematically have line of sight to enough revenue for any given timeframe to match your given capacity. If you have annual contracts with clients, bunch the renewals into the same period, if possible. This creates efficiency in the renewals process.

After reading through this chapter, if you find you are mismatched on your revenue and capacity, it's up to you to design your organization to solve the problem. If your capacity availability is out of whack, then you may need to "deepen your bench" and establish junior, senior, manager, and owner roles where you can place your revenue production. If the predictability of your revenue generation is out of whack, then it may be time to invest in that side of the business to create more defined revenue streams. Either way, investment is often needed to keep a scaling organization balanced and healthy.

This list of the seven revenue-planning considerations highlights how important the type of revenue you have is and how it can affect the capacity output of your team. But how do you know what kind of revenue is coming your way, really? Or, I should say, how can you predict it with any kind of reliability? All the following functions can help you know the future revenue that is coming in your door:

- Track your marketing (which is approximately 5 percent of expenditures on the P&L of a service organization). Is it converting to leads?

- Track your leads. This is where you begin to bucket them into different types of capacity needs. What is the percentage mix of small, medium, and large leads, or recurring, project, or maintenance service leads, et cetera? Is your leads pipeline enough to make up for team members you anticipate leaving or new hires you want to make?

- Track your MRR. Is your concurrent revenue covering your average monthly operating expenditures? Do you have new upcoming recurring expenditures that may change this mix, meaning you'll need new recurring revenue to make up for the additional expenses?

- Track your ARPC. Is your mix of revenue per customer too high (i.e., too risky)? Do you need to bring it down to manage the complexity in your service? Is it too low and your labor is not efficiently producing a high enough amount of profitable revenue?

- Track your client churn. If your client base is large enough, a churn rate can be worth tracking to know if the churn is shrinking your client base over time. Knowing if your client base is shrinking (i.e., net churn with clients coming in and leaving) will help you make decisions about your current capacity or the need for future capacity.

- Track your annual revenue divided by your client base count. Do you have 800 clients that produce $1 million in revenue? This is a low-complexity, high-volume model of revenue production. Do you have 75 clients that produce $2.5 million in revenue? This is a high-complexity client base, likely with high friction in client service and high reliance on seniors, managers, and owner. Both require different types of capacity and different ways to manage that capacity usage. Knowing which you are tells you what type of capacity you need to have available on your team.

You can know your revenue, the future planning of your revenue, and how it is affecting your capacity planning. Don't miss this important part of managing your service organization as you grow. This knowledge is more important as you scale larger. Service organizations that try to scale without having a handle on some basic tracking of capacity and revenue balancing can hit walls and not know why. This leads to real frustrations for the owners trying to grow.

In addition to knowing your revenue, you also need to remember the following:

You can't just hire any kind of capacity you want. Hiring is related to the anticipation of future revenue fulfillment. You have to hire in ways directly related to how you plan your revenue, and not just hire the people you meet who you think would be great cultural fits on your team (although that is extremely important).

You can't just take in any kind of revenue you want. We've alluded to this previously. Selling clients certain types of projects, whether one-time or recurring deliverables, has everything to do with who has capacity on your team to fulfill that revenue. If you take in revenue that only the owner can fulfill, that can have negative effects on growth as the owner steps away from growth and into revenue fulfillment. If you take in revenue that a struggling team member has to fulfill, you put that revenue, and your agency, at risk.

Much about scaling a service organization is about balance. We are all balancing where we are at any one moment in our growth trajectory, and it will always look different for each founder/owner. Your choice of the revenue you need is a balance of what you want and what your team can provide. As you grow, keep this balance in check so your growth doesn't go off the rails.

We did a lot of work trying to understand our revenue in this chapter. Now we'll explore the human side of our teams and how to track capacity. Let's dig in!

6

The Complete People Equation

Without a formal capacity plan, we were ultimately throwing people at problems. Proper capacity planning aligned with a profitable business model is the reason we're around today. Without it, you're running a glorified Ponzi scheme where additional headcount substitutes for sustainable progress.

CHAD DAVIS
(CO-FOUNDER OF LIVECA; 60 EMPLOYEES)

YOU'VE ALREADY MET Chad and his partner, Josh, who founded LiveCA out of Toronto, Canada, growing it from 2 people to over 120 in a decade. Their firm became an award-winning global leader while operating entirely remotely—so effectively that Chad spent over seven years working while traveling North America with his family in an RV.

Even from the very beginning, Chad and Josh understood the importance and power of capacity planning. As they moved through the scaling plateaus of 30, 50, and 80 employees, the rigor and importance of capacity planning became much more important.

There were countless spreadsheets, software products, exploration, and pontification; they leaned into capacity planning like no other firm did. So we asked Chad why. He told us this:

> Capacity planning is the basis of our business model. Combine that with standardized and structured pricing, automatic annual renewals, and a team that believes in the model, and you have something very special. But don't think it appeared overnight. We know we'll never be done, and it took over a year and a half to start seeing noticeable results.

We're going to attempt to plumb the depths of human capacity in this chapter and teach you here what it took years for Chad and Josh to learn on their own.

Capacity Value Striads

Jason Blumer

We know deep down inside that the CEO's time should not be used to fulfill the needs of a small recurring client. We know this in theory, yet we don't always practically apply this important principle when determining human capacity. Our first concept in this chapter will help us to see what capacity the CEO—and everyone else on a team—should devote to revenue production. This first concept is called capacity value striads (CVSs), and it can help us visualize where to devote our capacity. Let's look at how the CVSs are visually displayed within a tool called the Team Structure Capacity Chart (TSCC).

Capacity Value Striads

Team Structure Capacity Chart

Owners	Executive	Director		Manager	Senior	Team/ Other
		Organizational				
		Service				

Our chart is blank, but it is meant to be completed with boxes that each person fulfills in their role (you can see a sample filled-out TSCC on the book's website). That box represents not only that person's side of the chart (located on either the organizational or service side) but also the striad they go in on the chart: executive, director, manager, senior, or team/other. We'll continue to discuss how to use this tool for clarity of capacity usage for your whole team. One note: When consulting with service organizations, we avoid counting ownership on the TSCC. Ownership is included at the top of the chart but is not part of any capacity calculations. Ownership is a legal designation, and it relates more to tax filing, tax planning, and legal authority rather than to determining human capacity. We do, however, prefer that a legal owner also be included in their role location on the chart, whether it be executive or director. Listing an owner in a striad lower than director can cause confusion about who is actually leading the organization.

To provide context for our TSCC, here's a quick word about geology. "Striation" is a geological term for the grooves in a rock's surface caused by a variety of geological processes. We've adapted this concept for the "striads," much like geological layers, that should be formed in all service firms. For example, when a service firm is small, there is typically an owner layer and the individual contributor's layer (which we call "team/other"). Just two is all you need—not much geology in that. When you grow, you add more layers—striads—to support a more complex business. The striads are intentional, as you'll see. Which employee is in which striad, who moves into one striad and leaves another when being promoted, et cetera—it's all part of the strategy of adding struc-ture to the landscape of your expanding service organization. In a sense, we are adding fissures to your team chart to bring clarity to your company as you grow. Striads, or the formations resulting from striation, are something you build into your firm intentionally, whereas strata, mentioned in Chapter 3, represent different levels of team size.

The TSCC can help us striate our team's capacity at its appropri-ate level of value, including the leader/executive's capacity. Similar to managing an accountability chart, made popular by Gino Wickman in the book *Traction*, you are meant to place the roles of *all* team members in your organization on the TSCC in the correct striad. This means documenting your organizational chart by roles (and your employees' names) on the TSCC to visualize who is doing what across your organization. This helps you identify and define roles closer to how capacity is being used.

For example, a person on your team who is performing two separate roles needs to be placed on the TSCC twice, in two separate boxes. They might spend 50 percent of their time completing direct client work while also spending 50 percent of their time acting as the firm's billing administrator. You would create two roles placed in the right locations (e.g., service and organizational departments) on the TSCC. We divide their capacity in half to split them across the roles, while denoting one role (client service) as 100 percent revenue focused and the other role (organizational) as zero percent revenue focused. In addition to the striation of capacity, you'll also note that the TSCC has two distinct sides, the service side (revenue generating) and the organizational side (non-revenue generating), which we've already alluded to. This highlights a couple of key points about your team's capacity:

- All humans have capacity.

- But you are not using every team member's capacity to produce revenue.

This truth is big—maybe bigger than you realize at first read. The people you use to produce revenue are a strategic choice. Since you are unable to use all humans in your organization to produce revenue, you must choose very specifically which team member's time is devoted to aspects of growing the company that do not produce revenue and how much of their time is allocated to revenue generation. If you choose poorly, then you may have the least efficient team member producing revenue, thus affecting the profitability of your firm. And when you choose to pull a person out of client service, you're expressing a belief that their capacity is best used to serve the growth and support purposes of the firm, rather than to produce revenue. If you get these strategic team placement choices wrong, then you could be limiting profitability or have a sludgy operational department and not even know what is causing it.

Never fear. We are going to help you solve these problems.

Back to geology. You may have more striads than shown in our example, reflecting a larger, more complex organization, or you may have fewer striads for a small service organization. Let this chart be a guide as you build your own striated organization. Once you've placed each team role on the TSCC in the correct striad and on the correct side of the organization, then you can determine if the capacity usage by each role fits within the revenue production ranges we'll discuss next. Adjust these percentages up or down depending on your own organization's reality. These striad benchmark ranges are meant to guide how much of the team member's capacity is being used for revenue generation. This is the point of the TSCC—to visualize how your team capacity is available for either revenue production or growth and support of the structure you are putting into your firm. We discussed the importance of managing your revenue in the previous chapter, and now we are making general determinations as to how much of each value striad should be used to generate revenue and what parts of the striads should be used for non-revenue generation. We'll come back to these CVSs after an extensive example later in the chapter.

As a general guide, we want to provide ranges you can consider for team members in each striad benchmark. These will vary wildly between organizations since each firm's choice of team building will look different and each team member's commitment to efficiency will look different. Here are the guides you can use:

- Executive value striad = 20 to 30 percent (or less) of the executive's capacity to be used for revenue production

- Directors value striad = 40 to 50 percent (or less) of their capacity to be used for revenue production

- Managers value striad = 50 to 65 percent (or less) of their capacity to be used for revenue production

- Senior value striad = 65 to 75 percent (or less) of their capacity to be used for revenue production

- Team/other value striad = 75 to 90 percent (more or less) of their capacity to be used for revenue production

Remember, we are providing striads for firms of 50 team members or fewer. For larger, more complex organizations, we would expect the executive level to be closer to zero percent used for revenue production.

These ranges will help you visually plot your team on the striads and see how much of the team's capacity is being used for revenue production. Note also that these ranges are benchmarks. You can produce your own reality for your firm or agency based on which team is currently located in each different striad. Then compare your team's percentage of revenue production to the benchmarks on the TSCC to see what changes you may need to make to your roles.

If you find your team's revenue production is too high for their role location on the TSCC (usually within 10 percentage points up or down), then you would want to consider adding a striad to your organization or evaluate the role requirements. Our main goal is to make sure the correct striads are producing the correct amount of revenue. When revenue production is placed in the right striad, then the team can operate more efficiently (and remember, efficiency in service organizations is a driver of profitability). To aid in getting the right revenue production into the correct striad, we are always seeking to *waterfall down* revenue production from the roles in the top of the chart to the roles in the lower part. This allows the top part of the chart to focus on growth and strategy (high-friction roles) and the lower parts to focus on revenue production and efficient movement of deliverables (low-friction roles).

FRICTION

Any human-to-human contact involves friction. Sales, teaching, training, and consultative roles in a services organization are generally high contact and thus high friction, so service is slower. Where there is high friction, there needs to be a high-value component to justify it (like producing sales). You can design other roles to have less friction (i.e., less human contact); for example, junior roles and simple tasks. Low-friction roles should be able to accommodate high production volumes, with less judgment and assessment of data, and at lower price points.

Why do we approach the TSCC and striads in this manner? It comes back to the principles we learned in previous chapters. Like an accountability chart, the TSCC is a roles-based chart that is a visual representation of how your organization is designed and where your client service load and effort are placed. Furthermore, the TSCC clearly showcases where your expected production, management, and leadership capabilities exist. Are your managers overloaded? Is there enough (or too much) scaffolding to ensure proper management of the team? Have you placed the wrong person in a leadership role?

As an organization grows and adds more structure, there is more to manage, and more complex scaffolding needs to be applied to a larger organization (remember the principles of the Service Organizational Strata from Chapter 3?). The leadership striad is meant to manage the organization and participate in more of the future strategy required of a growing organization. If revenue production is not appropriately being accomplished by the right team member in the right CVS, then a firm could bog down and operate too slowly, have no leadership (since the leaders are producing revenue), fail to have managers that oversee the efficient production of revenue, and many other poor results. Organizational design isn't just about the management structure; it is also about the revenue delivery structure. Populating, maintaining, and tweaking the TSCC is a way to see how your capacity plans are working out, if they are at all. This is a tool for you to create, use, and continually look at how you intend to use your organization's capacity for revenue generation.

I'll take a moment here to point out how simple (and unhelpful) some of our traditional metrics of measuring a team's capacity are. We may ask each other, "How billable is your team?" and then smartly reply, "Oh, we like them to be between 70 and 75 percent billable." These statements fall short of what it takes to know the capacity of a team when you are scaling on purpose. There is so much more to the placement of a team in our company's roles, the measurement of capacity output for the humans that work in our organizations, and the continual changes and tweaking we must do to our machines to keep them operating optimally.

MELT

Obviously, no human can have 100 percent of their capacity used—we aren't machines. So we have to consider how humans respond to their work in different settings and seasons of their lives. This leads to the second key concept of determining human capacity. The MELT model of the human helps us to understand the employee's ability to focus on their job and be efficient in revenue production. MELT is the human's

- mind;
- emotions;
- location; and
- time committed to their work.

Mind encompasses their ability to focus and any mental or neuro-diversity issues, such as ADHD (which one of the authors of this book has), that affect their ability to focus on capacity output (whether the effect is good or poor). "I'm sorry, I was thinking about the *Godzilla* movie I saw last night. What did you say again?"

Emotions represent their ability to remain resilient during hard times, navigate their personal and professional complexities and the balance of their life and work, and appropriately regulate their responses to the people and the world around them at work. "My last kid just left for college this weekend, so I am a mess and not as focused on work today as I should be."

Location is an important component after the worldwide pandemic, and it could entail work in an office, in their home, while they travel, at an offsite location (like a coffee shop or client's office), or hybrid (sometimes in the work-directed location and sometimes remotely). "I'm not used to working here and forgot my second monitor at home. So, I think I just need to pack up and head back to my home office."

Time is what people have traditionally equated to capacity. We see now that capacity is much more complicated than just time, though time is a major component of capacity management. The time factor of the MELT model relates to the volume of their calendar that a team member is willing to devote to the company they work for. "I know you think I work part time, and my pay shows it, but I feel like I'm giving full-time hours to this company."

We can divide MELT into two different categories: *capacity trappings* that the human employee must manage and *capacity resources* for the organization to manage.

Capacity trappings are related to aspects of capacity that the employee controls. We label these "trappings" because issues of the mind and emotions, which we all have to deal with, can determine how effective we are as humans in our capacity output:

- Mind: What part of the team's struggle to focus is related to their mind, distractions, or inability to think clearly or consistently?

- Emotions: What part of the team's struggle to focus is related to their emotions, troubled lives/families, or general sense of anxiety or over-excitement?

Capacity resources are directly within the guidance and oversight of the organization and can be strategically managed by leadership using policies and stated protocols of service. We label these "resources" because, if used well, they can aid a team member in becoming more productive.

* Location: What part of the team's struggle is related to where they work, their environmental interactions, or inconsistencies of how they work at home or other designated spaces?

* Time: What part of the team's struggle is related to their time management; their failure to efficiently batch similar work; whether they are part time, full time, an employee, or a contractor; or their commitment to see their work through to the end?

In the previous section we placed our full team on the TSCC to reflect our entire company. Now we are going to give a score to each team member that represents their MELT. But before we do, a couple of thoughts on MELT.

First, much of what embodies a MELT score are personal issues you can't necessarily broach with a team member, like depression, aging parents, or their own mental or emotional struggles. So our assessments are applied to the team members as you hear them share or as you observe the issues. We are not insinuating that you must ask for this sensitive information in order to make an appropriate MELT score assessment. You are simply using this assessment in a way that gives you better visibility into the revenue devoted hours (we'll address these in a moment) you actually have available as a company.

Second, some have asked me, "Is it okay to make these assessments about your team without their knowledge?" To that I answered, "It's none of their business." You do *not* need the permission of your team to apply these intentional growth strategies, assessments, and calculations so you can scale your organization effectively and with intention. These types of assessments are part of the tool chest that managers, directors, and owners have to operate their service firms with as much intention, efficiency, and profit as possible. These are tools to make your capacity awareness and sophistication increase—use them!

Now we'll discuss how to map MELT for each team member on our second key chart in this chapter, the Capacity Analysis Chart. We'll give each team member what we call a MELT discount score, and we'll deduct a certain percentage from their work hours (represented by their salary) to represent what MELT is taking away from their total work hours.

MELT Discounting in Action

Let's say you have a senior team member who contractually works for you forty to fifty hours per week. For this example, we'll pick forty as the hours they are set to work, per their employment agreement. Currently, about 75 percent of their capacity is devoted to revenue production due to decisions by leadership. That means you are using 25 percent of their capacity for other things that you task senior roles within your organization. This may include process management, technical training, client issues to solve, role bridging (as discussed in Chapter 5), and dealing with difficult technical conundrums in your service.

In determining their salary ($90,000 per year), you are aware that only 75 percent of their salary is being used to produce revenue (in other words, roughly thirty "billable" hours out of forty—we'll discuss "billable time" in a moment). It's okay that not all of their capacity is being used to generate revenue, because a growing organization needs the senior-level team members to serve the organization. Now consider a particular human who embodies the senior role. Let's say this person is struggling in this season of their life with depression and is about to move to be closer to their aging parents. You need to think through their MELT and apply a discount to their capacity—a MELT discount score:

- Mind: They are generally focused, so you don't apply a discount here.

- Emotions: They have a lot going on, and you can tell they are struggling, so you apply a discount of 7 percent to their capacity.

- Location: They are going to be moving and trying to work during their move, so you apply a discount of 3 percent to their capacity.

- Time: They know how to calendar block and are generally self-managed, so you don't apply a discount here.

This senior team member, then, has a MELT discount score of 10 percent (M + E + L + T = 0% + 7% + 3% + 0% = 10%).

How do you apply the discount in a way that helps you track the team member's ability to produce revenue? The MELT discount is an intimate score of the human's loss of capacity, so the discount applies to all of their efforts while working in your company. It looks like this:

- Total hours in example above = 40 hours (or 100%)

- Total hours (minus MELT) = 40 hours × 90% (i.e., 100% – 10%) = 36 hours

- "Billable" = 36 hours × 75% = 27 hours (or 67.5% of a total of 40 hours)

- "Nonbillable" = 36 hours × 25% = 9 hours (or 22.5% of a total of 40 hours)

That means they are able to give you only 67.5 percent (27 hours ÷ 40 hours total) of the revenue-generating capacity they contractually agreed to. And this MELT discount applies to their nonbillable time as well. Since they agreed to work forty hours per week, for the foreseeable future you are getting only twenty-seven hours per week (40 contracted hours × 67.5% "billable") of revenue-generating time due to the MELT discount. Seems complicated, but this can be easily tracked in the Capacity Analysis Chart, a simple spreadsheet for the whole team that you can total by, for example, team member or department.

Revenue Devoted Hours

Instead of using the phrase "billable time," we'll use revenue devoted hours (RDH) in our calculations to note what we really have available to produce revenue. Many in the services professions are turning away from creating their revenue billing by the hour, so the "billable time" moniker applies less and less. We are also seeing that "time" is not a full and accurate reflection of what we've come to understand about our teams. The post-pandemic world has shown us that measuring professionals merely by their time output is a vestige of industrial thinking. It's a view that fails to capture the true depth of humans' contribution, their emotional intelligence, their deep creativity, their adaptability, and other dimensions that neuroscience has shown us are fundamental to how we solve problems and create value. We want to move away from time as being the only basis for how we assess and judge humans.

RDH is a team member's time, net of the MELT discount score. To continue with our previous example, the RDH for this senior team member is twenty-seven hours that can be devoted to revenue production, per our *unscientific* assessment. While you may have thought you had roughly forty hours per week of revenue-generating hours available from this team member, it turns out that you only had twenty-seven hours possible after factoring in that they are human, not a machine, and that they are contributing only 75 percent of their capacity to completing revenue-generating work.

How would you feasibly track this for a whole team? If you have a small team, you can easily track it in our Capacity Analysis Chart (which is just a simple spreadsheet). If you have a large team, then you would have department leads producing this data to be reviewed by directors.

Some of our senior/manager teams have noted that producing this data takes a long time. We remind them that an assessment is a quick update to the MELT discount score being maintained for our team. In a matter of ten to fifteen minutes, for about 12 to 15 team members, you want to either keep the MELT discounts the same from week to week for each person you are responsible for leading or change it when new information surfaces. This should not be difficult or complicated, but rather a quick unscientific scoring system to help your leadership see this new type of data at a summarized high level. The greatest value from this exercise will be the patterns you see over time for the same person.

Let's take our example and populate the Capacity Analysis Chart:

Capacity Analysis Chart

Capacity Value Striad (CVS)	Hours Paid, per Contract	MELT Discount	Hours, Net of MELT (100%−(B))×(A)	% of Time Devoted to Revenue	Revenue Devoted Hours (RDH) (C)×(D)
Column	A	B	C	D	E
Executive					
Director					
Manager					
Senior	40	10%	36	75%	27
Team/Other					
Team Totals					

Note: For ease of calculation, we have minimized this chart to be presented in a book. But you may expand your columns on your Capacity Analysis Chart to include more of the criteria you

want to track for your team (like the four specific components of
MELT, etc.).

Of course, we don't lower someone's salary just because they
move to take care of their aging parents, but due to their personal
choices, we are now getting less revenue production from this team
member for the same labor expense to the company. This is not a
perfect science, as no amount of managing a human team can be. In
fact, you could make the argument to shave 5 percent off every team
member's calculation for an additional MELT discount just because
they are human (especially including the founder/owners!). This
detailed example is simply meant to help you strategically place
the right team members in the right CVS and apply an appropriate
MELT score to their revenue production output. We are seeking to
bring some clarity and a new set of data to determine human capacity for service organizations. When you perform this calculation for
a whole team on a regular basis, you can begin to see patterns that
provide clarity on your team's available capacity.

So how do the Team Structure Capacity Chart, Capacity Analysis Chart, and MELT discounting models come together to provide
us with answers and visibility so we can know and plan our team's
capacity? By placing all our roles into the various striads, we can
better understand and calibrate what each person's revenue production output percentage is across the management levels of the
organization. Once you've got your Capacity Analysis Chart filled
out and have a rhythm in which you fill it out, then you can make a
judgment about where each person stands using the striad benchmark ranges introduced earlier in the chapter.

Now that we have a process for assessing our team, we can identify which value striad shows the biggest struggle for our firm. We
can calculate benchmarks for our team members related to their
capacity output, and we can begin asking questions to improve this
in various categories and identify why they are falling below the
guideline for their particular CVS:

- Our leadership: Where have we been unclear as leaders regarding their role and our expectations? We always start here when we want our team to improve their RDHs available for revenue production.

- Their leadership: Assessment of manager and senior roles often comes with some form of their own leadership requirements with other team members. Are they allowing the team they lead to bog down? Are they fearful of leadership, and are they directing their team accordingly? Do they need more training on how to lead their team to move work forward? Have they been given the right level of authority?

- Project management/efficiency: Does this team have the support it needs to remain efficient within the priorities we've assigned it? Where are the team members getting bogged down, and how can we help them be more efficient? Do we allow them to self-manage their own work too much?

- Scope definitions: Is our scope clear for the clients we have assigned to the team member? Are they struggling with navigating scope creep (where the client oversteps their scope and continually asks for more service) or scope seep (where the team member seeps out overservice that is not warranted by the client contracts)?

- Personal issues: Although personal issues are sensitive and we need to be careful approaching them, we can still fully expect our team to perform the role they have agreed to take. When they struggle consistently, their personal issues can be a distraction and hindrance to the work they have agreed to do.

A striad value range that is too wide can indicate an organizational design flaw that may need to be addressed. Once each role is evaluated and finalized, we can then move to evaluating each team member's individual MELT to further reduce their overall and revenue-producing capacity to match the reality of their unique situation.

It may seem like a lot of work to track a team's capacity, monitor RDHs within their CVSs, or measure their MELT on an ongoing basis. But this is what you signed up for as the entrepreneurial leader in a service organization (and we're providing spreadsheets and guides on our website to help you too). The owners and executives need to make these assessments for each team member on an ongoing basis (at least monthly, preferably weekly), and this is one way to note the patterns of the human data that may be affecting the efficiency of your revenue output.

To be clear, the MELT calculation is not something calculated by team members other than the managers and leaders. While your managers might inform you of the various situations surrounding your team members, the MELT is not necessarily a public metric. MELT is sensitive and specific to each team member, and it needs to be kept and managed in confidence with the higher management and leadership roles within the striad.

As with any organization, your management techniques will support you in your understanding and assessment of the factors affecting your employees. In fact, per our research, organization management has increased 9 percent from pre- to post-COVID, which is the highest-improving business competency tracked in the Practice Excellence survey. When we dig down further, the highest-improving operating mechanism, growing at 112 percent, has simply been the frequency of meeting cadences (called rhythms, as we'll note in Chapter 10). To understand your team, you need to invest time to get to know them so you can properly assess their strengths, opportunities, struggles, and productivity. That ongoing engagement will support you in your assessment of each team member's MELT calculation. Your first move is to get these tools up and running, then you will be amazed at what you begin to see and learn about your team and your organization.

Once you are done assessing each team member's MELT score, you have all the necessary components to properly calculate your organization's overall capacity over time, whether it be weekly, monthly, or quarterly—this includes each team member's total working hours, their RDHs, and their MELT score. You can aggregate your team's totals across roles and striads, in departments, and in overall company totals to get an accurate reflection of revenue-producing capacity over time for the whole company. As we'll see later in the book, we'll be using these calculations to conduct our various planning activities, including capacity planning and production planning.

Download spreadsheet templates you can use to make company-wide determinations of human capacity from the book's website.

So What Do You Do with This Information?

What now? First, ask yourself, "What is my next team move?" Service leaders should always be considering team moves, as the movement, restructuring, and clarifications of teams and their roles keep a service organization from becoming bloated, unfocused, and inefficient. This thought will also allow you to stay ahead of an unforeseen scaling plateau that may be sneaking up on you. If you are trying to expand your agency, there is always a team move to be considered. Do you want to use the calculations and principles in this chapter to turn your growing organization into a well-oiled machine? Here are some principles to consider.

Team chart visibility. All service organizations need to have a view of the location of their team on a chart. The chart is built with roles (not people) for the most effective movement of the team. Then humans are "hired into" those roles. We use the EOS Accountability Chart from the book *Traction* with our clients, as well as the Team Structure Capacity Chart from this chapter, to create this visibility. One is for accountability, and one is for productivity and team assessments.

Restructuring with team moves. Consider restructuring your team chart to move people into different roles best suited for them to match their capacity abilities. The goal here is to create efficiency in the use of their capacity, if possible. Is there anyone you can move on your team chart now?

Move sides: operational versus technical. This is moving team members from service revenue production to the organizational administrative side (or vice versa) to enhance a team's capacity abilities. For example, it is often wise to take a team member with technical proficiency in tasks related to revenue production and move them to a role that is less revenue focused, such as a project manager, an account coordinator, or an operations manager. Note that you are losing a revenue-producing team member when you do this, but if your organization needs what we call a "knowledge movement" role (like project management), then it may serve your whole organization well to promote someone from the technical side of your business.

Role types. Some roles have a propensity to becoming overwhelmed, and thus a poorer use of capacity in the company. In the TSCC, note that service roles are dedicated to revenue production and become less glutted over time than organization roles that are committed to the administrative side of the company. Why is this? Where revenue justifies the existence of a role, it is easy to note when someone is overwhelmed because of how much work you've given them. In this case, the level of revenue assigned is what signals whether a role is overburdened. On the other hand, roles dedicated to the administration and operations of the company often unknowingly become glutted because it's more difficult to note when someone has too much in their role (or that their role is too varied), since there is no revenue production associated with their role. It's wise to watch the organizational roles in the company so the administrative team members are not hindered from the efficient use of their capacity.

New role creation. Creating new roles is an innovative part of growing a service organization and works wonders to un-glut roles and create more efficiency. More efficient roles result in work flowing more rapidly through the company, thus creating more profitability.

Promote, hire, fire. Promoting, hiring, or firing team members can create greater efficiency and capacity usage. This can effectively reset the team member's focus and allow them to try to be successful and efficient in a new area of the company. Moving a team member to a new role also means they will adopt a learning curve, which may inhibit their efficiency for a time.

Peeling or combining roles. Peeling roles apart or combining roles can create efficiency. As a service organization grows, roles often become glutted. You may have to "peel" things out of a team member's role so their focus (and thus efficient use of capacity) can increase. You don't have to completely change their whole role, but you can pull things out of their role that may be better suited to another role as you grow. Or you can get better efficiency by combining things from multiple people's roles into one role. Further, you can create a new role, peel efforts out of two or three other roles, and then combine them into the newly created role.

Pack the capacity tighter. Move team members to full time. Move a team member from a contractor role to an employee. Or move toward a fuller capacity focus for a team member's role—meaning if they are at thirty hours of production but are full time, then move them closer to thirty-six hours of production. Humans fill up the amount of time given to perform their work (a summary of Parkinson's Law). Filling up their work to a tighter capacity can force them into a more efficient operating mode. Similarly, if you allow a *lot of room* in their capacity, you'll find team members incorrectly allowing a small amount of work to fill up a full-time role.

Remember that our goal in learning about human capacity is to optimize our organizations, use our capacity efficiently, and grow profitably and sustainably. Though optimization will always be the goal, it can never be completely achieved. Leading your team to be efficient is the job of the leader—we don't assume or expect our teams will work efficiently. Also, as leaders we care about our team. Our thoughts about them, our assessments, and our leadership ability to move things around are one way we care for our team. My partner and I love our team. We truly do. When our team is overburdened or struggling to do their jobs, this causes angst for us—not just because they aren't working to a full capacity, but also because they feel stressed and overwhelmed. We don't want them to feel that. So we must be wise leaders, make these assessments, and get better visibility and insights into how to lead our human teams with more care and intention.

The enjoyment of leading a service organization is in the journey to navigate the complexities, not some destination of being "fully optimized." Humans will always be human, and you as the leader are also always going through various seasons of life. You are constantly changing as a leader, and this can be the joy in our work. Embrace the journey instead of the frustration of feeling like you'll never arrive. You will never reach a place where you say, "Great, I have all the roles and the right team in place. I can grow profitably now!" You will always need to be applying the concepts and principles in this book as long as you lead a service organization. Enjoy your journey.

7

When Growth Gets Unexpectedly Complicated

Capacity planning is very difficult and complex. It's the consistency as much as it is the actual human elements. What happens when someone is sick for a week? And it becomes even more nightmarish when you are dealing with the surge of seasonal work.

MIKE LIBBEY
(PARTNER AND COO OF YBL; 37 EMPLOYEES)

FOUNDED OVER TWENTY years ago by Ross Libbey, Your Bottom Line (YBL) has gone through many changes to evolve and push through the scaling challenges it has faced. Whether it be from service realignment to succession planning to COVID to rebranding, the YBL team has overcome numerous challenges and roadblocks to move the business forward. As of the writing of the book, YBL has attained 35 percent in top-line growth for each of the past four years and is establishing itself as one of the fastest-growing full-service Canadian accountancies out of Toronto. But that doesn't mean everything is easy.

Managing the various complexities of scaling a firm is difficult. Mike and Ross face high seasonal demand, changing client needs, and cross-border complexities, while working tirelessly to hire, train, and retain a growing team. To manage these complexities, Mike says:

> We've done everything in our power to mitigate the seasonal surge. In addition, we look for people who are cross-trained as much as possible. We're lucky, as we've been able to find people with different talents and flexible skill sets to act as utility players when our client demands change.

But, as for many firms, managing their human capital is not only difficult but also strategically necessary. As they have grown, the little efforts they made early on have helped them succeed now and in the future. For example, during the seasonal surge, they use a buddy system, where a senior and junior staff member can work together to share the immediate items (like tax work), while pushing out and solving in parallel other work (like bookkeeping work), even though it was originally assigned to one person or the other. Mike suggests:

> Start with something that's basic and flesh out your capacity planning from there. Something is better than nothing. Don't let paralysis by analysis happen—otherwise you'll throw your hands up in the air and never move things forward.

Why Are Different Companies Different?

Ian Vacin

In 2017, I was presented with a challenge by my Karbon co-founder to develop a framework that explains why one service organization was successful over time while another was not. It was a simple challenge conceptually but difficult in execution. Over the course of a month, the Karbon Practice Excellence assessment was born and pre-tested, and now, for almost a decade, we have collected and analyzed data to understand how a service organization evolves and matures over time. Our goal was to measure the outputs and inputs of a firm. For the outputs, we didn't measure the quality of the work but rather its value, calculated as revenue per employee. For the inputs, we measured how the firm invested in the business side of things to understand where they spent time and effort to improve how they operated.

It took considerable time to build and analyze the data. As the data came in over the years, the information it provided was fascinating and thought provoking. Things weren't as simple as you might think. With a large data set, things didn't always show up as we expected.

In my prior life, I worked in manufacturing systems (semiconductor manufacturing, to be exact), where machines could be measured, shifted, tuned, replaced, upgraded, or even eliminated. Your outputs defined your inputs, and your inputs created your outputs. Results were predictable, explainable, and able to be modeled. But that just wasn't the case with the data set from service organizations found in the Karbon Practice Excellence survey.

But why? Managing humans and their capacity is no small feat. As a leader of a human organization, you know that each person is complex and complicated, as we discussed in the previous chapter. When you create an organization whose output is based on the collection of people working within it, the firm can be a mess to deal with. So while we dove deep on revenue and capacity in our last few chapters, now we are going to explore the complexities of human capacity that need to be accounted for at the macro level.

Jason Blumer

The fact is, people are different. Different from each other, and even different from themselves at different times. My partner and I, in our growing boutique advisory firm, are constantly working with our team to stay focused and lean into the commitment we've all made to the roles we've accepted. This takes training. Some team members have always lived by the calendar; others have never really learned to manage their time and need good leadership to keep them on track. Some days everything is running smoothly and everyone is working together and ready for more revenue work to be added; other days it's like a demolition derby on a frozen lake, and you're wondering, "Is that team member about to quit?" or, "Are we pushing them too hard?" or, "If they're struggling now, how much worse will it be with three more clients?" And of course, there are no answers, just anxieties.

But that's how it is when you're an entrepreneur: Every good day can be followed by a bad day. As soon as you get the structure all figured out, someone quits or you have to demote someone, or a huge client leaves and your ninety-day capacity plan is in the trash can. We're here to help you deal with and plan for this reality. It means working with the humans in your firm and helping them to stay focused on the task at hand and commit to the constant growth that is required of a firm optimizing for more profit.

Maximizing Firm Profitability

Ian Vacin

When Jason and I conducted our interviews with service firm owners, one line of questioning was asking them to identify the order of importance of (a) their clients, (b) employees, and (c) the shareholders/owners. Almost everyone confirmed that the owners were the last area of focus for them and that profitability was an outcome of having great client relationships served by amazing employees. The majority (around 80 percent) cited their employees as the number-one priority. The other 20 percent focused on the client relationships.

The difference between the two interview audiences—employee-focused versus client-focused—was driven by the scarcity of talent or customers in the service-based industry they did business within.

For instance, at the time of writing this book, accounting firms are facing a very difficult talent situation, while creative design agencies have their clients facing difficult inflationary pressures post-pandemic. As a result, the primary focus of a service firm will depend on current market dynamics, with the combination of employee and client foci driving shareholder success.

Why does the firm focus matter? Focus helps an organization deal with its complexities. Dealing with complexities helps a firm provide maximum value to its clients, which in turn results in maximizing the firm's profitability. Firm owners need to ensure they have the right clients served by the right team members, all working together using the right processes. These are the 3 Rs we introduced you to in Chapter 3: revenue, resources, and recipes.

In the next few chapters, we'll keep referring back to the 3 Rs Framework as the intersection of revenue (client work) and resources (team) that is supported, mitigated, managed, and optimized by the recipes (processes). When these are managed correctly, we have the right ingredients to ensure a well-managed firm that drives maximum profitability—the underlying goal of any service organization.

The Many Faces of Capacity

To fulfill the firm's revenue requirements, we must have the necessary capacity from our resources. We spent Chapter 6 looking at how to do this. If capacity is mismanaged through our overall recipes, then we experience over- or undercapacity, resulting in suboptimal profitability. At the end of the day, we have to actively manage a human-based system; the maintenance of our human capacity is critical to our success.

Running a service organization is complex and difficult. We will look in depth at five key areas of complexity where owners of these organizations struggle. We're not covering every possible situation or eventuality—how could we?—but we're laying the groundwork for a solid grip on the areas where you're going to encounter difficulties:

Market: Managing the changing market dynamics (and forces) to ensure you have the right revenue at the right time for the right team mix

Finances: Managing finances to ensure you have the resources to match demand while also ensuring the well-being of your firm and team

Environments: Managing where people work and how they collaborate

Operations: Managing logistics to ensure work is collectively done at quality and on time

Human resources: Managing the people themselves

Each one of these aspects needs to be properly planned and managed. These five aspects of capacity complexity exist in all firms, whether you produce widgets, tax returns, consulting projects, large websites, or custom commercial architectural renderings. However, the difference for service organizations is how the human workforce transcends all aspects of the firm and impacts capacity management across all facets. Like we said previously, it's complicated!

Complexity 1: Market

First, let's look at the broader impact of market forces and the firm's dependency on demand. Market forces are aspects we can't control, so we need to try to monitor and understand them so that we can put plans in place to minimize their impact. As we'll learn later, variability and uncertainty are two components we want to minimize. In some cases, we can control them, and in other cases we need to have plans in place to react to them.

Market forces exist in three flavors: demand-side, supply-side, and blended (both demand- and supply-side). Demand-side market forces come from the customer and purchaser of knowledge services, and they affect pricing and purchasing preferences. Supply-side market forces come from us, the entrepreneurs, as we produce our services, create the prices customers pay, and influence the price of services available in the market. Unfortunately, the first half of the 2020s gave us all three of these market forces, including a global event (COVID-19 pandemic), inflation (the fall-out from government pandemic spending and significant global economic disruptions), and resulting price changes (due to decreasing supply of talent that drove up prices for software, real estate, salaries, and much more). These blended market forces resulted in a very challenging work environment for service organizations, requiring lay-offs (and rehiring), raising prices of services, and outsourcing firm activities. While generating revenue was important in the 2010s, profitability has been and will continue to be more important in the 2020s and beyond.

In a service-based, knowledge-dependent organization, these combined market forces can't simply be corrected quickly, unlike in manufacturing firms. When markets go sideways, manufacturing firms can slow or stop production. Machines can run idle, and lay-offs can be performed. Disruptive? Yes. Recoverable? Yes. Costly? Yes. In a manufacturing business, there is often a greater abundance of labor you can hire and train. Machines that build the widgets can be easily turned back on, modified, or purchased to do the work based on the demand requested and production schedule required.

In a service business, 45 to 50 percent of the firm's total revenue is traditionally spent on human capital (calculated per the US Census, when comparing industry-reported revenue versus payroll). However, those costs have risen post-COVID, with two-thirds of firm owners confirming a rise, per our quantitative survey. Today, an average of 49 percent of total revenue is spent on human capital due to many factors, such as hybrid work environments and flexible work contracts (e.g., outsourcing and fractional workers). And this labor cost is rising still. Knowledge-based businesses live in a world where there is limited good talent to choose from. While lay-offs might be the answer for manufacturing businesses, they aren't a simple answer for service organizations. Key team members will undoubtedly be difficult to find and rehire later when you need them. It may be better to "take the financial hit" and have some team members work less *in* the business and more *on* the business. In other cases, it may even mean having them remain idle for a period. As we all know, the cycle of business is one of ups and downs, and as the owner, you need to navigate that cycle successfully.

HUMAN CAPITAL

The economic value of your people, based on the experience and skills they bring to your organization plus their productivity. The more experience and skills they provide, the higher potential value they can generate per job. The higher their productivity, the higher quantity of work they can complete over a given period.

While blended market forces are less frequent (thankfully), demand- and supply-side market forces are consistent threats and headaches. On the demand side, we face issues like changing small-business needs, changes in competitor pricing and offerings, technology shifts and trends (did someone say AI?), and changing economic conditions. On the supply side, we face issues like changing costs (labor, software, fixed assets), technology, government policy, and human capital productivity (personal and natural events), plus increased demand for specialized labor.

In demand-side market forces, we need to be most concerned about the factors that drive demand variability from our clients, which can be disruptive and fatal to a firm. As we discussed in

Chapter 5, we need a clear understanding of current and future revenue so we can plan and deploy our resources. Optimal profitability means having the right production capacity to match demand. If we overpredict our demand by not considering adverse market forces, we can be left with higher costs and lower revenue, which could turn our business upside down. As the owner of the firm, you are responsible for this.

We've found that in the past few years, slowing and stagnant demand has resulted in unused capacity, which eats profits. And in a service firm, this isn't overstock sitting in a warehouse, it's your employees collecting a salary for playing *Minecraft*. When this happens, many firms think it's a great time to put these team members to work on new market niches or new revenue streams. I'm sorry to tell you that Jason and I have both tried this and had very poor results. If you want to expand to new markets, consider it while also maintaining your current market concentration—this is a less risky way to consider new markets. We did this at Karbon in 2017, moving our software's focus away from accountants and over to small businesses in general. It was the only time in the history of the company that we had stagnant growth. Nine months later, we realigned to focus again on accountants, and we returned to world-class growth.

Many entrepreneurs feel the weight of having too few clients, so they try to get new clients anywhere, even by expanding into new markets. But this could stretch your human capacity, dilute your message to prospects, and ultimately not provide the benefit you were hoping for. Remember, the team you hired matches the clients you serve and the services those clients need and want. Moving into a new market direction (demand) typically requires different resources to make it work well (supply). It takes time to build the structure needed.

Now let's quickly look at supply-side market forces. I'm sure you're acutely aware of these. Talent is increasingly difficult to attract, hire, and retain. And labor seems to get more and more expensive. Technology that we depend on to run our firms also gets more expensive, and we need more and more tools to efficiently lead our organizations. Other costs continue to rise as well. And then, our team members have life events (babies, marriages, divorces, deaths), while natural disasters seem to increase around the globe. All of these are the supply-side market forces that we entrepreneurs must navigate.

As time marches on, the work seems to take people longer to perform than it should. To get something done just feels harder each day. New hires seem slower. It's frustrating, especially since we know what needs to be done and it feels like we could get this all done quicker if we just had the time to do it ourselves. Unfortunately, we all suffer from what we call "entrepreneur disenfranchisement." It is a combination of three factors resulting from the complexities of growth:

- Diseconomies of scale: Due to ineffective scaffolding, the business is less efficient, with higher costs, slower operations, and decreased profitability.

- Organizational drag: Increased numbers of bottlenecks slow down profitability and innovation because of outdated processes and increased bureaucracy.

- Corporate sludge: The culture shifts and productivity decreases as you add more people and scaffolding.

As the Notorious B.I.G. wrote, "Mo Money Mo Problems."

All of this stems from the struggles of managing a service organization that depends on humans to complete the work. Without our employees, we don't have a business. With them, we feel firsthand the struggles to work to create a productive and profitable business. While we can't control supply-side market forces, we need to be aware of them no matter how painful that might be. We need to stay on top of what our competitors are doing or saying. We need to understand the market rate and availability of our various roles and resources. We need to try to minimize the number of systems and curtail the rising costs of technology. And we need to plan for the expected unexpected happenings to lower our team's productivity by tracking and managing MELT. These are things we can do to make us more informed and construct alternative plans as things inevitably go sideways or upside down.

Complexity 2: Finances

The second area of complexity is finances. We have unavoidable constraints in capital holdings, free cash, and departmental budgets. In any firm, "cash is king." I hear firm owners say repeatedly, "If we just had the capital to do this, we would be so much further ahead." But that isn't reality when you're running your own business. And, as a counter example, the US government handed out cash with seemingly no strings attached during the early days of the pandemic through the Economic Injury Disaster Loan program. This was available capital, yet we are seeing now that most clients maxed out these loans and used up all the cash, while the underlying organizational mismanagement was simply masked by the availability of the loans. So access to capital is not always the easy solution we hope it is.

We need to find, win, deliver, and collect on the demand (new revenue) while matching the supply (new or more efficient team) to ultimately end up in a favorable profit situation. In a growing firm, we typically reinvest that newly won profit into resources and recipes that can drive increased future revenue. As a result, our capital is consistently constrained, so we need to be thoughtful and efficient in how we use it.

As we've seen in some detail already, to make things more complicated, service organizations serve other businesses who have their own financial-capacity constraints (e.g., your clients' clients). This leads to chasing clients who are also struggling for outstanding receivables and seeking to eliminate and prevent their own delinquent debtors.

A goal without a method is nonsense.

W. EDWARDS DEMING

_____

And there is another major cost center: technology. Technology is implemented to support the other pillars of capacity, but it is a growing cost that limits our financial capacity to do other things.

At Karbon, we conducted research pre- and post-COVID on the average technology spend (as a percentage of revenue) by accounting firms using the Practice Excellence survey. Pre-COVID, Karbon recorded that firms spent around 6.4 percent of their revenue on technology. Many publications and industry experts had reported the total anywhere between 5 and 7 percent. Post-COVID, Karbon measured that the average accounting firm spent 7.8 percent of its revenue on technology, reflecting a 22 percent increase from pre- to post-COVID and possibly reflecting firms' increasing investments in AI-related products. During our interviews with the owners of other service firms for the book, the same sentiment was shared that regardless of service-based industry, technology spend as a percentage of revenue has increased since pre-COVID times. Our quantitative research for the book showed that technology spend was in fact 9.5 percent on average across all industries sampled. Regardless of the amount, the increased expenditure on technology means there is less free capital floating around to commit to other growth activities.

With our financial situation constrained, we need to focus on the revenue we do have. While we discussed earlier that we can find more demand, we can also be more efficient and thoughtful with the revenue we are already bringing in, beyond being better at accounts receivable collections. Lots of revenue and resource capacity is lost in three key ways: ineffective pricing, scope seep, and scope creep.

Pricing is literally a book in itself, so we won't go into depth on it here. Firm owners know they need to be bolder and more thoughtful in what price they ask for from clients, and they need to move from time-based billing to value and higher fixed pricing to maximize the outcome for all parties involved. Suffice it to say that your skill at pricing directly impacts the amount of revenue you bring in, so pricing is a paramount topic for the success of your organization.

For context from our survey, firm owners report that

- 17 percent are pure value-pricing firms;
- 41 percent are a mix of value pricing and fixed-fee pricing;
- 31 percent are mostly fixed-fee pricing; and
- 11 percent are mostly time billing.

We've alluded to scope seep and creep before, but I want to add a deeper discussion here, as this is directly related to the management (or mismanagement) of your revenue.

At Thriveal, Jason has taught for years on this topic using the concept of the Capacity Exchange Bridge. In this concept, revenue from clients is exchanged with capacity from the team. On the client side, we receive revenue and in return give clients our team's capacity. On the team side, we exchange payroll for the capacity our team members give us. As owners, we are on a bridge, so to speak: We go to one side to give payroll to our team to purchase their capacity, then cross over to the other side and exchange that purchased capacity for the revenue we want our clients to pay us. It's a constant exchange, back and forth, and it all has to work in concert or one side of the equation may become too high or too low, depending on how you view it.

What protects this capacity exchange is what we call "scope." Scope is the contractual definition of how much of our team's capacity we will give to our clients in exchange for their revenue. We seek to give no more and no less than what has been defined in the contract with the client (which is why we like to say that every dollar earned in a service organization should be documented with a written contract). Scope is what brings clarity to the earning of the revenue. In a sense, if your team's capacity is your inventory, then scope is your forklift in a service organization delivering the goods to the client. It must be managed with intention.

As we consider this bridge that owners and leaders stand on and the complex work we do to keep both sides working optimally, we must be mindful of two ways in which capacity can be lost. Though the bridge is where the capacity exchange happens on both sides of the equation, the problem happens under the bridge, so to speak:

- Scope seep: Often without the service-organization owner knowing, scope is seeping out through overservice of the contract. The team does more work than they should or than is contracted for the revenue being paid.

- Scope creep: Often without the service-organization owner knowing, scope can also be crept upon by the client asking for more and more service. Scope then creeps past the capacity the firm had agreed to give to the client in the signed contract.

The result of mismanaged scope can be an insidious loss of capacity, and thus revenue. In both cases, scope seep and creep, the organization should have asked the client for more revenue to justify the overservice. A failure to manage the contractual definition of scope, both scope seep and creep can lead to financial constraints that are hard to see or control.

Complexity 3: Environments

Over the past decade (and accelerated due to COVID), the workplace for knowledge workers has shifted from the office to working fully remote to now working in some sort of hybrid. While current trends show the pendulum swinging more toward being in the office, we will now and forever get our work done digitally—both where we choose to do it and how we get it done. Our work is done fully on computers, our office can be wherever we want it to be (perhaps three days a week in the office and two days a week at home), and we collaborate with our colleagues through online tools rather than in face-to-face water cooler conversations.

With everything now online and our work patterns increasingly remote, running a firm becomes even more complex. It is difficult to know who is where, what they are doing, and when things will be done. While you used to be able to swing by a team member's desk to say hi or have a quick discussion while grabbing a coffee, now your team might be halfway around the world, providing you with a very short overlapping window for a formal meeting. Your team might constitute a mixture of

- full-time employees (and they may be in-person, hybrid, or completely remote);

- part-time employees;

- outsourced workers;

- fractional experts;

- seasonal workers; and

- gig workers.

In a 2025 Karbon study, growing accounting firms stated that they hire through a mixture of arrangements, including (in percentages) full-time employees (61 percent), part-time employees (32 percent), outsourcing (30 percent), and fractional/seasonal/gig workers (14 percent). (Multiple selections were possible in the study due to firms hiring various types of resources, so the percentages do not equate to 100.)

For service organizations, physical capacity (a sub-component of environmental capacity) has been relatively relaxed as in-office arrangements have become less favorable. With people now in hybrid work situations, the in-office constraints don't exist like they did before. However, this can affect productivity. There needs to be a discussion on using tools, techniques, and technology to enable collaboration between staff and clients, since in-person dialogue is difficult or impossible. We might also bring in the impact of a remote team that is located in different time zones or different countries, or even outsourced altogether. Culture becomes an issue in this regard; it's an important focus to cultivate in your firm, as we highlighted in Chapter 1. Productivity is typically corrected and driven by the culture. Lack of physical proximity in a digital environment means you have to be even more intentional about your culture. You can't "see" bottlenecks, understand dependencies, and mitigate accordingly. There is no longer a paper trail in the office; it is now a digital audit trail. Therefore, the coordination of resources becomes much more difficult as well.

In Chapter 10, we'll look into operations management techniques like rhythms and reporting, which will help solve these environmental capacity issues.

Complexity 4: Operations

When we talk capacity, complexities, and constraints, most people gravitate to the operational side of things where, defined from our revenue, we have work to be done that will be completed by a defined pool of resources. In the operational area, our recipes are critical for making sure that our resources are productive enough to complete the work on time. Recipes combat variability in our processes and people, and they give us confidence in the face of project uncertainty, which we will look into in depth in the next chapter.

As I have learned over the past ten-plus years building a software company that directly supports service organizations in their quest for operational efficiency, the majority of firms (54.9 percent, per the Practice Excellence survey) don't have more than just their core processes documented, and nearly half (45.3 percent) don't update a process more than once a quarter. Is that you?

Your service organization's processes are your intellectual property. They are the key thing that enables your team to perform their work fully, repeatedly, consistently, and with excellence. When you combine your processes with the right talent, you instantly have a strong probability of successfully delivering the work to your clients at or above their expectations. Without well-documented processes that your team is trained on, you have little hope of meeting those client demands and expectations. As we'll see in more detail later, we need to build, document, train, and continuously improve our full catalog of processes to obtain competitive advantage not only against our competitors but also against the forces working against the team itself, manifested in team inertia, individual laziness, and misguided effort.

Since I started working directly with service organizations back in 2002, I have often heard firm owners say how excited they are for some new technology and observed their misguided expectations about how it would solve their wildest issues. I founded a tech company, and I know that technology isn't *the* thing to solve your problems. Most likely, the thing that will solve those problems will be your processes. The technology you wrap around those processes will act as an accelerant. If you add it to a high-performing system, tech will improve efficiency, productivity, and delivery at a lower cost. Add technology to poor or non-existent processes or an underperforming team and you'll quickly find yourself in a worse position than you were before, and with less money to show for it thanks to the technology investment.

Time is a critical consideration, especially in the operational area. Time creates complexity. The further a future time is from the present, the more uncertainty it holds. If you have a task to do today, you feel more certain of what to do, how to do it, and when it will be completed—this is what we've called the understanding of *concurrent* capacity. But if it's a longer project, perhaps three months in length, are you certain on when to start, how to do it, how the project will go, and when it will actually be done? You can't predict with certainty whether the people you depend on for the project will be there, if the requirements of the project will stay fixed, if people can complete their tasks as quickly as projected, or if the way you planned to solve the problem will be the best path forward. In Chapter 11, we'll use a variety of planning tools that span different time horizons to manage the operational complexities that time throws at us.

Complexity 5: Human Resources

Our last area of complexity is our workforce—our resources. This is not just the humans themselves but also the organization that supports them. Much of this book is about these human complexities. In the next chapter, we'll be looking at the specifics of firm complexity related to growing human capital. We have already looked at other human-related complexities:

- Resources, our supply, are increasingly more expensive and less abundant.

- Technology will become part of our resources, and it will eliminate redundant and low-skilled work.

- Human capital is subject to personal and natural disasters.

- Entrepreneur disenfranchisement highlights that an increasing number of resources don't result in a linear addition of capacity and productivity.

- Hybrid work environments and digital work create new challenges in productivity and management.

- Organizational structure and design are critical components in creating the "scaffolding" necessary for a successful firm.

One area we haven't discussed that is critical in MELT assessments is the roles, tasks, and skills that our workforce must bring. This is about not just the bodies on our team but also the activities our workforce can complete and how flexible they are across the variety of jobs to get the necessary work done. Winning is a team sport in small business. While someone, maybe you, might be amazing at defining a brand, completing a tax return, drafting a legal trust, strategizing over a large media buy campaign, or advising a client on an acquisition, the collective work of the firm needs to get done. That might include getting samples, collecting documents, getting signatures, or printing a report—all things outside of the scope and skills of your star employee, who might be amazing at a particular facet of the business but can't possibly do everything. Our *utility* players who are versatile and adaptable are perhaps the most valuable on the team.

UTILITY PLAYER

This type of labor on our teams enables us to use capacity most efficiently. A utility player's flexibility to perform various roles across the organization allows for capacity gaps to be filled at the expense of profitability, while ensuring client satisfaction through timely revenue delivery.

Let's use some analogies from basketball and baseball to make the point. While the 2015 Golden State Warriors were winning championships in the NBA with the Splash Brothers (Steph Curry and Klay Thompson) dropping threes and Draymond Green controlling the paint, Andre Iguodala was coming off the bench to support the defense and offense in whatever way he could. While Aroldis Chapman was getting saves, Jon Lester strikeouts, and Anthony Rizzo and Kris Bryant homeruns on the 2016 Chicago Cubs baseball team, Ben Zobrist was getting hits and playing both infield and outfield to help the Cubs win the World Series. Both Iguodala and Zobrist were given the MVP award during their championship series for their contributions and were instrumental in winning their respective championships.

Don't get me wrong: Our most skilled team members typically drive higher margins by either delivering our high-revenue services or working at high levels of productivity. But these resources, in time, also become expensive. We don't want them doing office admin work, chasing debtors, crunching data, or doing manual data entry. But we need that work to be done, and we need players on our team who are flexible enough to do both low-skilled and high-skilled jobs efficiently and cost effectively. This is what Mike was talking about at the beginning of the chapter. The utility players are and will be extremely valuable when we do our short- and medium-term planning, which we'll discuss in Chapter 11. As a service organization owner who probably prides yourself on client service, you never want to miss a deadline. These utility-player team members are the puzzle pieces that ensure our projects make it out the door (hopefully) on time, on budget, and at quality.

So cross-training and upskilling our team is important for providing our business with the flexibility to get the job done. However, the "retooling" of our staff can be quite challenging. First, training takes time, which typically isn't available. Second, it takes a willing staff member to embrace change and learn a brand-new role. And third, it takes capital to provide the training and pay for the increased salaries of these employees as they become more skilled and capable. Perhaps that is why, per the Practice Excellence report, internal team training is the number-one factor that separates the leaders from the laggards. It isn't easy. But when done, and done repeatedly, it provides excess capacity so you have the flexible resources required for dynamic planning. As we'll see later, that flexibility is critical in countering the uncertainties we face each day when running a successful business.

Running and growing a service organization is complicated. It isn't just the clients we serve and the services we provide that make it complicated; it's managing a whole host of factors—market, finances, environments, operations, and human resources—that can seemingly come out of nowhere to set us and our businesses back. We'll dig deeper in the next chapter to understand what the root drivers of these complexities are and what factors influence them so we can properly address these complexities in the last part of the book.

8

Taming the Inevitable Chaos

Our guideline is that we move the work rather than the people because we want to try and keep our people working as a team.

JOANNA BOWLES
(COO OF SAYER VINCENT; 109 EMPLOYEES)

ASED IN the heart of London, Sayer Vincent, a 109-person audit firm focused on nonprofits, has progressed through numerous scaling plateaus over the past forty years. With up to nine-month-long audit projects that require specialized knowledge to complete, Sayer Vincent has had to be creative to manage difficulties in scaling, capacity planning, and finding people to do specialized work.

In the management of the firm itself, Sayer Vincent has evolved the organization scaffolding to encompass a four-tiered technical structure, facilitated by an operations team that runs all administrative support. The structure is made up of the C-suite (partners), department managers (audit managers), staff (leveled by skill), and trainees (new grads). Of the 109 employees, 8 are in senior leadership, 26 are in operations, and 75 are in service delivery, organized in hubs of 23 people per team. In terms of capacity planning, Sayer Vincent's goal is that for every 78 client audits, they need to have 9 trainees, 2 managers, 1 partner, and 1 client services coordinator in the associated hub. Leah Matthews, operations manager of Sayer Vincent, told us this:

> We approach capacity planning from two angles: first, how we align our existing people with the timing and volume of current work; and second, how we forecast the future workforce we'll need to deliver what's coming next.

To satisfy the large, unmet market demand while operating in an extremely limited talent pool, Sayer Vincent decided to create its own robust training program. Now at scale, Sayer Vincent takes on ten new fresh graduates and career changers every six months to build the expertise needed to satisfy the resource demands of the ever-growing hubs. Once the trainees graduate to fully qualified staff members, they continue to hone their skills to get further promoted across numerous levels in the staff tier, from which they might later be promoted to audit manager. The continuous focus on training and upskilling has resulted in strong financial results, a positive work environment, and a culture that sets Sayer Vincent apart from its peers. As Jonathan Orchard, Sayer Vincent partner, said:

> The next step is about strengthening our culture, making space for smarter, more efficient ways of working, and growing with purpose, not for the sake of it. That brings together how we want to move forward. Our training and structure are the engine that drives our success.

The Undercurrents

Ian Vacin

Now that we have explored some of the biggest facets of capacity complexities, we need to understand the undercurrents that drive the complexity in our 3 Rs. In any given system, there are two nemeses we must always seek to minimize: variability and uncertainty. These can dismantle any well-designed and well-intentioned system by directly impacting a firm's quality and the timeliness of its deliverables, eroding or destroying profitability. Firms spend countless resources to combat these forces. For variability, we track time, develop standard operating procedures, train staff, create reports, optimize processes, purchase technology (e.g., practice management), and more. For uncertainty, we perform discovery work, create packaged services, simplify proposals, narrowly define the scope of contracts, niche, cross-train staff, hire more mature workers, conduct reviews, and more.

Variability and uncertainty create a vicious circle in service organizations. Variability in the inputs reduces confidence in our capacity models, leading to uncertainty that then drives over-hiring—ultimately reducing profitability. To break this cycle, we must define all elements of capacity with precision (as we have discussed in great detail in the preceding chapters). This is why we've evolved beyond simplistic measures like weekly hours or billable time allocations. Instead, we analyze capacity through the MELT framework at the individual level, while using a Team Structure Capacity Chart to visualize capacity distribution across the entire organization. This all becomes further complicated by the firm owner's mindset.

MINDSET

An owner's mindset is developed over time, and often the owner is not aware of the mindsets they are operating under. Being unaware of mindsets can lead to managing and leading in unknown ways. Their mindset can find them operating *automatically*, which is counterproductive to being intentional as a service firm leader. Growing owners are open to having their mindsets challenged by people, communities, and other owners/leaders they trust.

If the firm owner's mindset is conservative, they may over-hire to ensure demand is met (possibly out of fear), lowering revenue per employee. If the owner is aggressive, they will under-hire and over-work their team (possibly out of neglect), obtaining high revenue per employee in the short term but possibly increasing employee turnover and negatively affecting culture over the long term, which will stifle the firm's growth. Both lead to suboptimal profitability and a poor culture in the long run. In our quantitative survey, 65 percent of firm owners classified themselves as aggressive and 35 percent as conservative. We want to be in the Goldilocks zone—not too conservative and not too aggressive. We accomplish that by managing variability and uncertainty through proper and thorough measurement and management. As we'll learn later when we discuss planning and reporting, we use differing planning horizons (and methodologies) to combat uncertainty and variability over time.

Many factors influence variability and uncertainty in service organizations, but we'll focus on three of them, which encompass the past, present, and future:

- History
- Firm complexity
- Time

Factor 1: History

Each of us has a journey line. As a firm owner and entrepreneur, you have two that are intrinsically intertwined: one for yourself and another for the firm. As entrepreneurs, we often "get in our own way," and thus our own personal journeys make our firms' journeys that much more complex. The opposite is true, too, where the firm's growth can encourage the owner's growth personally. These two journeys are intimately intertwined. The journey through the ups and downs and successes and failures is the outcome of your decisions—both good and bad. If you don't learn from experiences, then the variability of your decisions will materialize in your future decision making. This is such a profound leadership lesson: Your work and outcomes can often be traced directly to decisions you made in the past or responses you had to situations. We can't blame anyone, but rather we should embrace the power we have to determine our futures.

If you continue to operate with variability (i.e., being unintentional), you'll likely have the same percentage of ups and downs for future decisions you'll need to make. However, as your firm grows, the number of challenges and decisions you face will undoubtedly increase, resulting in more ups, more downs, and higher swings as you seesaw through the future. The past predicts the future, and your intrinsic variability will make your journey feel like a bumpy speedboat on rough waters rather than a catamaran gliding across the ocean. Design your service organization and you will counter the chaos inevitably found in variability.

So, the question from your history is this: What have you learned, and how will you respond when the next curve ball comes at you? For me, my journey line had a sudden shock in 1999 when the CFO of the company I worked for embezzled $3 million and fled the country. As a recent addition to the leadership team, I spent the next nine months helping to get bridge loans, only to watch as we laid off over a hundred people and shut down the company. From that experience, I learned how important finances, and the financial function of a company, are to the company's livelihood. That experience drove me to focus the remainder of my career on building financial software (Intuit and Xero) and founding a company (Karbon) dedicated to supporting the heroes of finance—accounting firm entrepreneurs. Since that moment, I have always watched the finances closely in my personal life, business career, and as an entrepreneur while seeking and hiring some of the best financial professionals to support me.

The more you experience, reflect, and learn, the better your decisions in the future will be. The more you invest in yourself, your team, and your firm to protect yourself from the missteps of the past, the higher the probability that you'll make decisions that steer your firm forward rather than backward. Those experiences, and more importantly your reflection on them, are what give you the confidence as a firm owner and entrepreneur to make the right decisions when you need to, which lowers both variability and uncertainty. In this case, your past influences the future—hopefully one with more highs and fewer lows.

Factor 2: Firm Complexity

Firm complexity is inherited. It comes from the decisions, both good and bad, that you make along the way as an entrepreneurial leader. Firm complexity can be influenced, mitigated, and managed. It is the outcome of increasing revenue serviced (who we serve plus what we provide) by increasing resources (who does the work). In other words, the more work you have to do and the more people the work requires, the more complex it becomes to coordinate activities to ensure the work gets done as planned.

This concept of firm complexity is exacerbated by the prevailing belief of service firm owners and entrepreneurs that bigger is better—more revenue, more clients, and more staff equal business success. Jason and I hear this often as we go to conferences, run events, oversee roundtables, coach owners, consult to turn around firms, and meet firm owners across the globe. Firm owners will size each other up by asking how much revenue they make, how large their team is, and how many (and what) clients they serve. Consequently, for most firms, complexity manifests itself in increasing firm size, breadth of services, and diversity of client base. That is not to say complexity is guaranteed to exist in all cases. Some firms are able to keep complexity under control as they grow. We'll explain how in this section.

Service organizations are human-based systems, and humans are complex and unpredictable, so the larger everything becomes, the more complex it is to manage. In our research for the book, we met with firm owners who had grown into the first scaling plateau (8 to 20 employees) and would say things similar to what Jennifer Green from Jade Consulting said in the quote we opened this book with:

> When we were smaller, I knew what everyone was working on. It was manageable because of the size of the team and the number of clients. Now we're approaching 15 employees, and my biggest struggle right now is that everything I thought I knew, I don't know anymore.

Jason and I have also faced this with our own businesses. As my company, Karbon, grew from the founding team of 8 to now over 300 people, we went through the same scaling plateaus (18 employees, 40 employees, 65 employees, 150 employees) and management shifts (from 3 founders to a 12-person executive team) that you will experience when you grow. There have been multiple times during this journey when I questioned what I was doing and wondered where our business was headed. I too had the same voice in my head as Jennifer. One lesson I learned from my experience founding Karbon, as I compared it to my other startup and scaleup experiences, is not to underestimate the power and impact of a strong and positive firm culture to combat complexity. Your culture is your foundation and guiding light as your firm grows and evolves.

Have you had similar thoughts? If so, don't worry; you aren't alone. The simplest solution is the age-old advice of KISS—keep it simple, stupid. That is, managing an ever-growing system of variability and uncertainty requires us to attack this complex issue with the simplest solution—one that often turns out to be the optimal solution too.

Let's dive deeper to understand this in more detail.

Balance complexity with scaffolding. As we've said before, the larger your team, the more scaffolding you need to support it. Even at 8 or 10 employees, you will need a small layer of management. As the layers of management grow, this creates more inefficiency, which in turn generates both variability and uncertainty. Just think of it in simple terms like the telephone game. The more management there is between the decision-maker and the individual contributor, the more the message changes and the intentions of the message are misconstrued. But you can't have a flat organization either—at that team size, a flat organization is no organization. The larger the team, the more you need to develop formal processes, train your team on them, and spend time on reporting to understand where your most important commodity—time—is being spent.

Interestingly enough, I was able to provide evidence of this from applying a regression analysis to our Practice Excellence data set. A regression analysis lets us understand the relationship between an output (Practice Excellence) and its various inputs (like tools, reporting, management techniques, etc.) and by how much those inputs can predict the output when applied. When we conducted the regression analysis, it identified the top three factors (in order) that separated high-performing firms from low-performing firms:

1 Formalized staff training programs

2 Workflow management software

3 Reporting of "jobs completed by staff"

As I said earlier, as your firm grows, so does its complexity, which will be managed through necessary firm scaffolding.

Simplify the who, what, and how of servicing clients. The first and second components of the key factors of uncertainty and variability (history and firm complexity) are both related to servicing clients. The more revenue we agree to earn—the more services we provide clients and the more kinds of clients we serve—the more complexity it creates in the resources and recipes we need.

As both Jason and I witnessed during the pre-pandemic era, there was an underlying sentiment in service-based industries that growth was the measure of a firm's success. The more you did and the larger your firm became, the more revenue you would generate—and thus more bragging rights. But revenue is not the same as profitability, which, as we have established, is the true measure of success.

As we moved through the pandemic (both during and after), the Practice Excellence research interestingly showed that firms became more focused with their revenue and resources—what clients they served, what they did for those clients, and who they had within the team to do the work. More specifically, we saw flattening growth moving from pre-COVID (45 percent) to during COVID (46 percent) to post-COVID (46 percent), and increasing management scores of 50 to 51 to 52 percent, respectively (driven primarily by a focus on the organization management competency). During COVID, accounting professionals saw no shortage of work, and managing their resources became all that more difficult. We also saw increased efficiency (from 56 to 59 percent) and strategy (56 to 58 percent) scores, corresponding to how firms adjusted to combat firm complexity by investing in their recipes. As we dug in further, the competencies that showed the greatest increases from pre- to post-COVID were technology (9 percent), business processes (7 percent), and operations management (7 percent), and these are all part of the efficiency category in the Practice Excellence score.

When times get tough, firm owners have to respond to navigate the uncertainty. During an unprecedented time of difficulty, it was all about survival. That is when what is truly important surfaces—doing more with less. It may mean providing fewer services to a wider variety of clients (focused service delivery) or more services with fewer clients (focused client delivery). In fact, I have listened to Jason speak for decades about niching—providing fewer services to fewer clients. Rarely is the answer to profitable growth providing more services for more clients. Again, the simple principle of KISS applies.

Factor 3: Time

As we will discuss in Chapter 11, time is a vector that brings more uncertainty the further out we look. The closer to the present, the more we know and the more confident we are. The further in the future, the more options, paths, and decisions there are and the more uncertain we become. Time can't be influenced or changed, but it can be planned for to mitigate its influence on uncertainty.

Risk mitigation is a wise response to the complexity we find in the variance of time. That is, the further out we try to plan, the more we need to mitigate the unknowns of that planning with risk protection. Saving three to six months' worth of average operating expenditures in a savings account is a way to mitigate the risk of planning to hire a new leadership role out in the future.

So how do we combat variability and uncertainty through the various factors they present themselves within? We do so through better knowledge of our people, our business, our customers, our industry, and the world around us. In the next chapter, we are going to look at how to combat variability through the lens of operations management, and in Chapter 11, we will look at how to combat uncertainty through various aspects of planning.

PART III

EXECUTION

&

VALUE

9

The Decisive Operations Edge

*When you set a price, do all the work, see revenue
go up, but then profit go down—you have a problem.
Our operations weren't fulfilling the demand like we expected.
That is when all those inefficiencies in your firm come
into view. At that point, I made the decision to
take two steps backwards to take four steps forward.*

DAVID DINARDO
(CEO AND VISIONARY OF ENVOLTA;
35 EMPLOYEES WHEN ACQUIRED IN 2022)

ENVOLTA WAS FOUNDED in 2012, and it was generating $1 million in revenue in early 2020, when its CEO, David DiNardo, made the unheard-of decision to stop all sales and marketing. Running a completely virtual full-service accounting firm with 25 employees and built on a subscription revenue model, he just wasn't making a profit.

To get more clarity, the Envolta team broke it all down—from the business level to departments to the individual and then to the work itself. They shifted departments to pods, with each pod responsible for $1 million in revenue. Then, each individual in each pod had their own revenue target to hit based on their role, level, and capability. Victoria Peters, retired COO of Envolta and Gauvreau, explains:

> We were able to put the right people together, matching personalities and skills. We moved from departments of 12 people to hand-picked pods of up to 8 people. The right clients were then matched with the right people. And, most importantly, we focused on quality controls, training, and communication.

In terms of operations management, Victoria started with a self-review checklist for every client deliverable. It gave the team ownership, transparency, and an opportunity for training. As Victoria says, they wanted people who desired to expand their knowledge and grow. The checklists evolved over time, per the team, to quality reviews whereby a half dozen client deliverables were randomly selected and reviewed for each staff member. Each review would get a score, and the pods and staff would compete for the best scores. The teams would celebrate the wins and provide training to team members when required. As Victoria said, "We weren't afraid to try. If we can make it better, let's make it better. Everyone had a voice."

In regard to operating mechanisms, David posted a three-to-five-minute video every day on what was happening internally, externally, and with clients, which the team would comment and collaborate on. The team had weekly forward-looking meetings on Mondays, plus daily scrums (a scrum is a short, time-boxed meeting where the team synchronizes their work and plans for the day). The management team led town halls every three weeks. The collective mechanisms were rhythmic. And the Envolta executive team was open, transparent, collaborative, and empathetic.

As a result of the changes in operations management and meeting rhythms, in two years Envolta went from $1 million to $3.5 million in revenue while increasing staff by only 40 percent. David told us:

In retrospect, I wish we had put this in place on day one. When everyone has the same vision, instead of focusing time and energy on change management, you can focus time on delivering value to clients and generating business growth.

Getting Your Team Running Smoothly

Ian Vacin

When our revenue is defined and our resources are fixed, then our recipes are the answer to increasing our profitability. At the intersection of our resources and recipes is the area of operations management. Operations management is the art of helping your team work as efficiently as possible with all the operational rhythms, processes, and software needed to run an effective organization. A key part of success is managing your organization's human capital well. Envolta provided an example of how to level up operating mechanisms (which we'll cover in Chapter 10) to create a more efficient, and profitable, organization.

According to our Practice Excellence research, the US Census, and our quantitative survey, human capital in professional service organizations will be 49 percent of your total revenue on average, while the technology you leverage to make them more productive is another 9.5 percent of your total revenue on average (metrics we've mentioned previously). Our people are our major investment, and we need to maximize their productivity to create and maximize profit.

To best maximize our resources and profitability, service firms need to incorporate and understand four interconnecting methodologies of operations management:

Four Methodologies of Operations Management

Methodology	Purpose	Role	Definition
Total Quality Management	Manage quality holistically	Foundation	Establish a firm-wide structured approach to deliver consistent quality, improved efficiency, and best-in-class client service.
Lean	Eliminate waste	Mindset	Deliver continuous process improvement and increased enterprise value by minimizing eight categories of waste.
Six Sigma	Reduce defects	Process	Measure, standardize, optimize, and refine firm processes systematically to reduce variability and increase quality.
Operating Mechanisms/ Rhythms	Execute consistently	Management framework	Provide the necessary structure and accountability to monitor and sustain improvements in Total Quality Management, Lean, and Six Sigma.

Together, these concepts create maximum firm profitability by driving better quality of client deliverables at lower cost with faster delivery—more predictably. Although you may not become an expert on these concepts by reading this book, we will teach you these concepts in enough depth so you can grow in a more intentional way. As you read through these concepts, consider how they may apply to your own situation as you scale your service organization.

At the beginning of this book, I mentioned my "why" for writing it. After over thirty years of work experience and over twenty years working in the accounting tech sector, I never thought my journey would bring me back to what I had spent years learning, researching, working, and perfecting—industrial engineering and operations management. Before Lean and Six Sigma were corporate buzzwords, I was deep in the production and supply chain worlds building systems that managed the operations, reporting, and planning of semiconductor manufacturing plants at places like IBM, Intel, and Analog Devices. My pedigree includes

- a bachelor's degree in industrial engineering and operations research;

- two years of academic research at UC Berkeley studying arbitrage in sports, commodities, and currency exchanges;

- an APICS certification (before Lean and Six Sigma certifications existed);

- six-plus years in high-tech manufacturing and supply chain management;

- a master's degree in engineering management;

- Green Belt certification in Six Sigma; and

- co-founding and leading Karbon (practice management and workflow for accountants) for over ten years.

Let's dive a bit deeper into the world I love for each of the terms we mentioned previously.

Total Quality Management Is a Team Sport

Stemming from the teachings of quality pioneers from the 1950s (such as Crosby, Deming, Feigenbaum, Ishikawa, and Juran), Total Quality Management (TQM) is a management system for client-focused organizations where "employees continuously improve their ability to deliver services of particular value." TQM has eight guiding principles by which a firm is to operate: client focus, leadership commitment, employee involvement, process approach, continuous improvement, fact-based decision making, collaboration and communication, and integrated systems. The details of each are outlined below.

TQM Principle 1: Client focus. The goal of the first principle, client focus, is to deliver value by meeting or exceeding client expectations. This is accomplished by collecting and analyzing client feedback, monitoring satisfaction, and completing frequent check-ins with clients. Tools often used to complete this include the following:

- One-on-one client feedback sessions
- Voice of the Client
- Customer satisfaction surveys
- Net promoter score

TQM Principle 2: Leadership commitment. The second principle is focused on fostering a culture of quality through strong, clear guidance. This requires that leadership defines quality objectives, allocates resources, and leads by example in quality initiatives. This typically results in activities such as these:

- Mission and vision statements
- Strategic planning
- Quality objectives (via objectives and key results [OKRs])
- Leadership training
- Team meeting communication

TQM Principle 3: Employee involvement. Employee involvement is all about empowering all employees to own and contribute to quality improvement. This is accomplished through the organization providing training, encouraging participation in decision making, and celebrating contributions to quality improvements. When it's done correctly, you'll see activities like the following:

- Cross-functional teams

- Brainstorming sessions

- Employee surveys and feedback systems

- Recognition and rewards

TQM Principle 4: Process approach. For any efficient system, processes are critical to its success. The process approach's primary goal is to optimize workflows for consistent and efficient outcomes. This is accomplished by mapping workflows, analyzing process efficiency, and establishing clear procedures for consistency. Tools used include these:

- Standard operating procedures (SOPs)

- Documented processes (e.g., process flowcharts)

- Workflow checklists

TQM Principle 5: Continuous improvement. While viewed by some as a buzzword, continuous improvement is an important and meaningful principle. It seeks to drive ongoing refinement to identify, adapt, and excel. This includes a regular review of processes, identification of inefficiencies, and implementation of required changes to remove those inefficiencies. Activities that drive this cycle of change include the following:

- Plan-do-check-act cycle

- After action reviews

- Critical path analysis

- Root cause analysis

- Process-walks

- Benchmarking

TQM Principle 6: Fact-based decision making. This principle ensures that there is proper rigor (e.g., using data) in making important decisions. This includes following the necessary steps to gather data, analyze trends, and base decisions on measurable insights. Tools used include the following:

- Statistical process control

- Control charts

- Fishbone diagrams

- Pareto analysis

- Hypothesis testing

TQM Principle 7: Collaboration and communication. To ensure alignment and teamwork across the organization, the seventh principle fosters teamwork, establishes clear communication channels, and encourages information sharing. Things driving collaboration and communication include the following:

- Team-building exercises

- Communication plans

- Rhythms (e.g., daily standups)

- Collaborative tech tools

TQM Principle 8: Integrated systems. The last principle strives to align all functions to work cohesively toward organizational goals and to establish a unified quality management system. The purpose is to create an integrated system by which every person and system is rowing in the same direction to achieve a key objective. Systems and tools used to support this include these:

- Practice management system (e.g., Karbon for accountants, Clio for lawyers)

- Knowledge base

- Balanced scorecard

- Performance management

- Total productive maintenance

To get you more familiar with TQM, let's paint a picture using an analogy with your closest team—your family. While this example doesn't focus squarely on quality improvement, it does highlight efficiency improvement and how the eight concepts work together to generate a preferred outcome.

Imagine you are sitting at your desk working when a real estate notice comes into your inbox advertising your dream home in your ideal location. It looks beautiful! Built twenty to thirty years ago, a ranch-style home in great shape, but… it is just a bit outside of your affordable price range. That night, the family is together, and you have a discussion with them about the house. Everyone agrees it is worth pursuing. Everyone also understands, however, that it will require some sacrifices. You put down the bid and get the house, and now you are living in it. Congratulations!

However, as with any home, you have a slew of expenses and unexpected repairs. Now the home is definitely more expensive than you had anticipated, and you need to cut your costs. In a review of your finances, you notice that your utility bills are one of your largest (and growing) expenses. By reducing them, you could save that extra bit to cover the unexpected monthly overruns (plus, they seem higher than what you paid in your previous home). So you pull everyone in the family together and you say to them, "We are committed to reducing the cost of our monthly utility bills within the next year by 25 percent by being more resource efficient as a family."

As a result of the meeting, you ask your family to take actions that can reduce your consumption of electricity and say that you would love to hear some ideas on how best to save. In the short term, everyone agrees, and the thermostat is set lower at night, the heater is used less throughout the day, and everyone is diligent about turning off lights when they're not in a room. Since you are impatient to get your monthly utility bill statements, you end up conducting weekly readings of your outside water and power meters just to anticipate the savings. Unfortunately, even with all that, when the monthly bills come in the family notes that while you are saving money, it's not enough to reach the 25 percent goal by the end of the year.

So, as a family, you decide to understand how your utility bills compare to those of your neighbors, since all the homes in the neighborhood are similar. Your children learn from their friends that your water bill seems significantly higher than several of the neighbors' bills. Instead of just focusing on reducing the power bill, as a family you now pursue lowering the water bill too. Everyone takes shorter showers, you reprogram the sprinklers to go twice a week rather than three times, you no longer wash the car in the driveway, and you make the difficult decision to not flush the toilet after number one. Big sacrifices. You check the water bills, and again they are dropping, but not as much as expected. While thinking about what to do while lying in bed late one night, you hear the toilet running while everyone else is asleep. Aha—leaky toilet! You call a plumber, get it fixed, and voila... the next water bill is lower than the neighbors'. You met your cost reduction goal in six months' time, and your lower utility bills get you back into what you can afford monthly. Congratulations!

How does this example relate to TQM? Let's dissect the story according to the eight principles:

Client focus: The desired outcome was your family's ability to live in their dream home. While not exactly the best example of a client, your focus was, selfishly, your partner and kids.

Leadership commitment: Deciding to buy the house and selling that decision to your family was the first example of leadership commitment. The second example was clarifying to the family that they needed to commit to a 25 percent utility bill reduction to meet the affordability requirement.

Employee involvement: Everyone was committed to sacrificing for the dream house. The efforts made to save money, the ideas contributed, and even the family celebration at the end are all examples of employee involvement.

Process approach: Procedural orders such as turning off the lights when not in a room and flushing only after number two are examples of refined processes to support the defined goal.

Continuous improvement: The continued efforts to lower the power bill, re-evaluate all bills, and then refocus on the water bill are examples of continuous improvement toward the overarching goal.

Fact-based decision making: Using benchmarked data to home in on the water bill, plus the observations that identified the leaky toilet, show decision making based on observed facts.

Collaboration and communication: This was demonstrated by the various family meetings and the family review of the utility bills each month.

Integrated systems: While not much tech was used, the weekly review of the outside power and water meters and the adjustments to the thermostat and sprinkler system show changes to the home's integrated systems.

As the example highlights, TQM is a holistic approach to quality and efficiency improvement. To make these big, sustained improvements over time, you need the support of a well-coordinated and well-trained village. Leadership needs to be client-obsessed; create and sell a vision; give employees the necessary training, space, and trust; and equip the organization with the right reporting, fair decision making, and systems to be successful. Employees need to honestly support the vision, mission, and purpose of the company; have empathy, curiosity, and excitement for the clients; feel safe, trusted, and empowered; agree on the desired improvement outcomes and celebrate success; drive and value a collaborative work environment; and feel confident in their skills and tools to get the job done. All of this centers on a culture that both the leadership and the employees must cultivate together.

Total Quality Management provides the foundation for firm-wide process and quality improvement. Lean and Six Sigma are the joists and framing of our house of efficiency. With that, let's lean into Lean.

Redefining Lean Thinking to Work in a Service-Based World

Lean, Lean Thinking, and Lean Manufacturing were originally developed by Toyota in the late 1940s and further researched and labeled as Lean by John Krafcik in 1988 and James Womack and Daniel Jones in 1996. At its heart, the Lean methodology strives to eliminate waste and deliver continuous process improvement.

When looking at Lean, you will quickly notice its focus on manufacturing. Things like "idle equipment," "material movement," and "raw materials" just aren't concepts in a service organization. But don't worry—we simply need to redefine the eight waste categories and apply techniques to empower a service organization to succeed with Lean.

As defined by the acronym DOWNTIME by Jean Cunningham, the eight waste categories of Lean are as follows:

Defects: Errors, mistakes, or non-conformance in a product, requiring rework, repair, or replacement.

Overproduction: Producing more than what is needed or earlier than required.

Waiting: Idle time when people, processes, or equipment are waiting for inputs, approvals, or the next steps to begin.

Non-utilized talent: Failing to use employees' full potential, knowledge, or skills.

Transportation: Unnecessary movement of materials, products, or information from one location to another that is non-value added.

Inventory: Excess raw materials, work-in-progress, or finished goods that are not immediately needed.

Motion: Unnecessary or excessive movement of people, equipment, or machinery that doesn't add value.

Extra processing: Performing more work beyond what is required or valued by the customer.

Transportation, inventory, and motion don't directly apply to our human-based service organizations, so I have altered these and redefined the other wastes to be more relevant to us:

- Defects: Errors, mistakes, or incomplete work on a service job that requires rework to meet firm quality standards.

- Overproduction: Doing more than what was initially agreed upon (e.g., preparing or repeating work more frequently than needed) or completing work without a signed engagement letter.

- Waiting: Idle time when people or work are waiting for inputs, reviews, or the next steps to begin. Includes underperforming queues in just-in-time service delivery.

- Non-utilized talent: Failing to use employees' full potential, knowledge, or skills. This includes using high-skilled labor for tasks that should be performed by lower-skilled labor.

- Teamwork: The friction of collaboration, where valuable time is lost asking questions, getting answers, having meetings, and getting assistance.

- Information: Long overall project completion times due to wasted time and effort to find and retrieve information needed to get tasks done.

- Management: The production time lost because of poor tracking, prioritizing, coordinating, and managing people to get their jobs done.

- Extra processing: The team performing more work beyond what is required by scope (scope seep) or valued by the customer (scope creep).

With these new definitions, you can drive activities that eliminate waste and deliver greater efficiency in each category. Here are some examples:

- Defects: When mistakes are discovered, take the time to provide one-on-one coaching or have the staff member retake internal training.

- Overproduction: Ensure the team is properly brought up to speed on the details of the signed engagement (via a kickoff meeting) and that the engagement document and project scope are easily reviewable in their work management system.

- Waiting: Ensure work is visible, prioritized, and easily accessible with a protocol in place to pass and notify when work is changing hands. Conduct bottleneck analysis to ensure there is proper staffing to support the volume of demand at each phase of the work.

- Non-utilized talent: As needed, upskill and cross-train staff to ensure there is more flexibility in who can do what. Continuously improve your production planning to ensure you have the right people doing the right work at the right time.

- Teamwork: Establish pods to provide more focused work delivery. Put in place policies and training around communication and collaboration for the team.

- Information: Use technology (e.g., work management system) to bring all the client data (such as communications, documents, and notes) into one place.

- Management: Implement reporting and rhythms (which we'll discuss later) to enable the team to be self-managed and aligned on what needs to be done.

- Extra processing: Train the team on your standard operating procedures (SOPs) for your client services, plus provide training on the ins and outs of client management. Ensure they understand the scope of each service that is to be delivered.

Lean has been traditionally referred to as Lean Thinking, and as such, it isn't a methodology to follow to obtain a certain goal (unlike Six Sigma, which we'll discuss next). Rather, it is a way of thinking in order to drive systematic reduction of waste. Lean is a mindset you want to foster in your firm to help drive a culture of continuous process improvement and operational excellence.

The Goal of Six Sigma

Lean can be combined with another operations management concept called Six Sigma, which was developed in 1986 by a Motorola engineer named Bill Smith. Smith observed that defects were the result of process variations, so he developed a systematic way to reduce them. By removing defects, Six Sigma strives to ensure a well-controlled process (measured by statistical process control charts) with minimal process variation. (The target result is fewer than 3.4 quality defects per million opportunities, which corresponds to a defect-free rate of 99.99966 percent—in other words, the specifications limit is six standard deviations—or six sigmas— away from the mean in a statistical distribution.)

Like Lean, Six Sigma comes from manufacturing, so it needs to be reimagined for service organizations. Unlike a manufacturing line with sophisticated, well-tuned machines, we run a production line of messy, complicated humans. As a result, let's be thoughtful about what we expect from our teams. They can't obtain a defect-free rate of 99.99966 percent. They can't be at 100 percent capacity. They will have days where they are performing below (and above) their average.

With that said, you still need to measure human productivity. Team members should be held accountable to a reasonable target. Team members *should* strive to be at Six Sigma. As an owner, you offered the team a specific job with duties, responsibilities, and expectations outlined in a contract. The team signed those contracts and promised to fulfill those obligations. So the goal is to achieve the most from, and with, the team, collectively from that agreement supported by great leadership, a central purpose or goal, and a great culture. While the team can't obtain Six Sigma, they can aspire to drive the highest level of quality through the lowest level of variability in their completion of your clients' end deliverables.

We want to follow the principles of Six Sigma to obtain the benefits of improved client satisfaction, reduced work delivery time, reduced errors, and improved work quality. The Six Sigma principles are generally defined as follows:

- Focus on the client: Align and measure processes with the client in mind.

- Identify your SOPs: List, prioritize, map out, and analyze workflows to pinpoint inefficiencies.

- Reduce variation: Minimize inconsistencies to ensure uniform quality.

- Empower your employees: Create a culture of continuous process improvement through employee training and ownership.

- Make data-driven decisions: Rely on your data, tools, and analysis to drive changes. Be thorough in your analysis.

- Be flexible: Change is hard. Accept, empower, and adapt to change.

If you take a Six Sigma course, you learn about the DMAIC approach to improving an existing process:

- Define: Define the problem, output, customers, and process.

- Measure: Collect data to establish a baseline for improvements.

- Analyze: Analyze the data to find the root causes of defects.

- Improve: Develop, test, and implement solutions to improve the process.

- Control: Control the process to ensure improvements are sustained.

With these definitions in mind, and over the course of the last decade while creating Karbon, I have developed a more detailed, ten-step approach applicable to service organizations for process improvement to move them from discovery, through optimization, reinvention, and delivery, and to automation. We call it the PEACE-MAKER process, and it is as follows:

Prioritize: Determine the process to optimize. Create a list of your processes, and prioritize (by revenue, volume, and least efficient). Unsure where to start? Start with a process that bothers you most.

Expound: Discuss the existing process as a team. Gather the team, conduct an intake session, write down the details, estimate time per activity, and map out the critical path.

Agree: Agree on what is success and how you measure it. Review why you chose the process to improve and your expectations for improvement. Typically, measure in terms of process time and quality delivered.

Chart-out: Map out your "as-is" processes (and variants). Write your processes, maps, and documentation for the most junior person on the team. This ensures nothing is missed.

Evaluate: Discuss variants and why they exist. Take notice of when someone broke the process. Uncovering why they did it and what they did leads to process innovation.

Missteps: Review all steps for inefficiencies. Conduct a process-walk if possible. Look at each step in the process and question it. Why do we do this? Can it be done differently? Is it needed at all?

Actualize: Create a "to-be" process with a sub-team. Think about the process differently. Rework and remap the process from the ground up. Create the processes, maps, and documentation to support your testing.

Kick around: Test the process (or at least the logic). Ensure the process is used a few times in real-world situations to see if it works and is an improvement on your "old way." If not, revise and test again.

Execute: Document and implement broadly. Remember, a process is only going to reach its full potential if it's adopted across your firm. Training is paramount. Create, document, and organize in a way that makes sense to your team.

Refine: Automate, iterate, or further optimize. Make an effort to go back and re-evaluate each process at regular intervals. Continue to monitor, measure, and tweak to get to optimal performance.

The goal of Six Sigma is to improve quality in our service delivery through reducing variability in our processes. It is a focused approach to evaluating, reinventing, delivering, measuring, and tuning processes to increase our clients' satisfaction while increasing firm profitability. It is an iterative process and is the impetus for firms embarking on a continuous process improvement journey. These are the high-level details; we won't go into the depths—that's another whole book.

Even though I co-founded a technology practice management company, I have said repeatedly at conferences, webinars, and events that the most important aspect in your service organization is not the technology you purchase but the processes you build. In a knowledge-based service delivery organization, your processes are your intellectual property! They are what makes your firm special and different from your competitors. They deliver your services, drive your quality, and ensure your profitability. As a result, they are one of the most important aspects of your business besides your people and culture. Using the PEACEMAKER process to build and refine those key processes is one of the biggest step-changes you can make to your overall business.

Moving Processes to Checklists

A practical area of operations management that you need to incorporate into your organization is how to take your newly invented (or reinvented) processes from Six Sigma and make them more accessible and usable by your team. For knowledge-based work, the best mechanism is to convert your processes into effective, practical checklists. Let's go deep for a bit here.

CHECKLIST

A simple list of tasks that enable the person completing the work to ensure they don't miss any critical steps in the process and their performance of that task is consistent with the rest of the team. Each task should be written similar to a "to-do" to ensure quick comprehension and easy task completion.

Checklists are important because they take complicated routines and make them simple and repeatable while reducing errors and cognitive overload. They provide simple accountability and instant, transparent reporting. While checklists aren't necessarily elegant, they are magical. As mentioned in the last chapter, workflow management software was the second leading contributing factor separating leading firms (top quartile) from laggard firms (bottom quartile) in Practice Excellence. Checklists are at the heart of these software solutions, and they are responsible for ensuring that the right people do the right activities at the right time in the right order so that your firm never misses a deadline and your clients receive their deliverables on time and at (or above) the client's expectations. As such, they are magical in the world of operations management. Atul Gawande writes that checklists "are efficient, to the point, and easy to use even in the most difficult situations. They do not try to spell out everything—a checklist cannot fly a plane. Instead, they provide reminders of only the most critical and important steps—the ones that even the highly skilled professional using them could miss."

Fortunately, all the work that was spent in Six Sigma to build, visualize, and train your team on your processes can be leveraged in building your checklists. In process mapping, you can create either a step-by-step articulation of the process or, more typically, an end-to-end process flowchart (like our example). These can be high-level (just raw steps) or detailed (showing ownership, phase/statuses, data input/output, time expected, logic, and more).

Example Process Flowchart

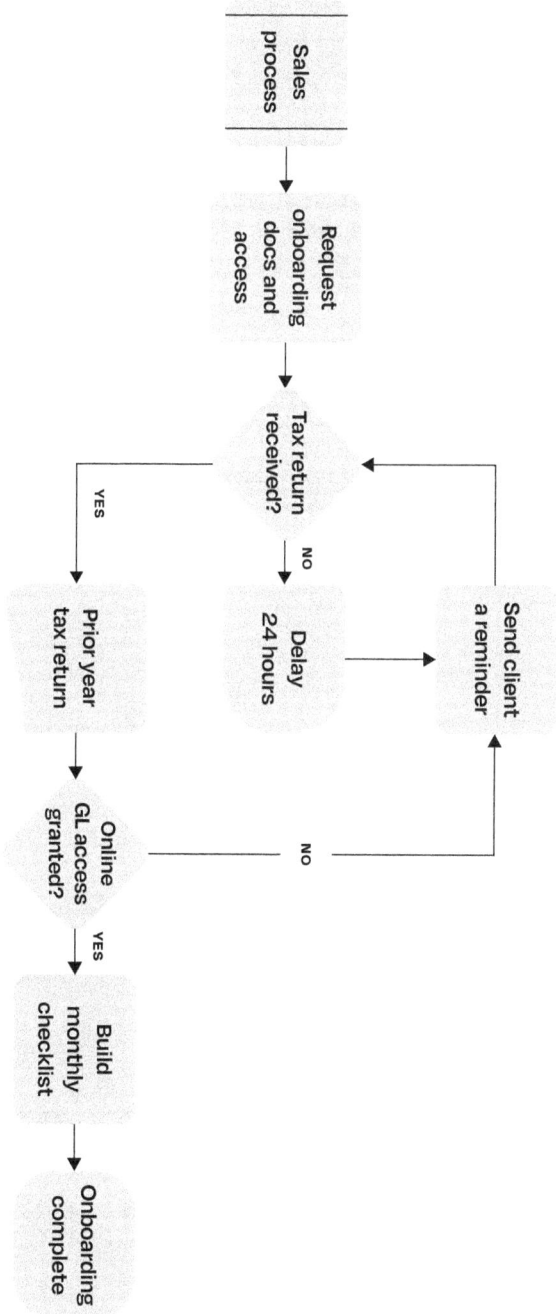

Once you have this, the conversion from process mapping to building the checklist, defining the related workflow (phases/status changes), and assigning the associated ownership becomes simple.

From Processes & Mapping to Work & Checklists

	Processes & Mapping	Work & Checklists
Raw data	Process name	Work template name
	Step title	Checklist item
	Step description	Checklist item description
	Step duration	Due date, budgeted time
Overview	Phase descriptions	Work status
	Subprocesses	Checklist section
Detailed	Ownership and notes	Step owner
	Order	Checklist step order
	Logic	Additional checklist steps

Now that you have the mapping, there is a simple pathway to create a practical checklist that your team can learn and use. From my past ten years leading Karbon, where I have had the honor of working closely with thousands of service entrepreneurs and operations leaders, I have developed the PLOW checklist methodology. It has four key components for checklist creation, and it reinforces the mapping logic mentioned above:

Particulars: Make checklist components generic yet specific to ensure they are flexible yet customized.

Lightweight: Keep checklists detailed enough to track yet lightweight enough to use.

Ownership: Give everything in a checklist clear ownership with clear hand-offs.

Workflow: For work to flow, bake visibility into the checklist.

To paint a picture, let's look at an oversimplified example of a new-hire onboarding process that I built years ago in partnership with Adrian Simmons, chief creative designer of Elements CPA. Here are some quick details of the process:

- Process: New-hire onboarding

- Objective: Move a new hire from "I want to join" to being a "creator of value"

- Goal: Improve the onboarding process from 90 days to fewer than 60 days

- Phases: Paperwork, proficiency, and culturalization

- Process overview:
  - [Paperwork] Step 1: Sign contract
  - [Paperwork] Step 2: Complete new-hire paperwork
  - [Proficiency] Step 3: Become proficient in the tools
  - [Proficiency] Step 4: Become proficient in service delivery
  - [Culturalization] Step 5: Model firm culture
  - [Culturalization] Step 6: Manage clients

CULTURALIZATION

The indoctrination of a new employee on a team, whereby over time they demonstrate through their actions the expected norms, behaviors, and participation similar to those of a long-existing team member.

Leveraging this example, let's explore each of the PLOW principles in more detail.

Particulars. These are the various levels of information you need to create so the checklist can exist on paper, in Excel, or in a workflow management system. This would typically be anything written as text in your process maps, plus some more detailed information that you would create when training a new team member on the process itself. The particulars include the following (from lowest to highest level):

- Procedures: The lowest-level instructions to complete a task (considered as the detailed training procedural steps). These are generally reviewed when someone hasn't yet been trained or has forgotten how to complete the step. This is written to support your most junior team member.

- Checklist item description: A high-level explanation of how to complete a given step in the process. May contain specifics on how to complete this step for a given client.

- Checklist item: The step or activity that needs to be completed. Usually there are multiple checklist items. A singular item would typically be referred to as a "task" and written like a to-do.

- Checklist: The entire set of steps (procedures) to complete a specific multi-step project. It contains a collection of checklist items and their associated descriptions and procedures.

- Work template: A checklist that has had its client-specific details removed so it can be applied to any given client. Due dates, budgets, assignee relationships, and more are left unassigned until the work template is deployed to become a checklist for a specific client.

Now, when translating this information from the process map to the checklist, be mindful of what information should remain generic (as it is in the process) and what information should become specific (to the client the checklist is applied to). Most service organizations want to provide a high level of client service and do so by having the client feel like what is being delivered is customized to them. Ensure the standardization of the process is married with the uniqueness of the engagement.

To be more precise, the aspects of the checklist that remain the same (generic) are the work template itself, the checklist items, and the procedures. The items that should be made specific in the checklist (for potentially every client) are the checklist overall (e.g., assignees, start date, end date, steps included, and order) and the checklist item descriptions. What that means is that every time you create a new checklist from the template for a new client, steps in the checklist may be removed (or moved) in order to reflect how the client wants to be served. In addition, the checklist item descriptions will also change to best describe how a given checklist item applies to a unique client situation, as it might differ from one client to the next.

Let's look at how this plays out in our example. For much of the new-hire onboarding process, the checklist items are going to be relatively the same. If we look at the first phase, paperwork, under the second sub-process ("Complete new hire paperwork") the step titles (checklist items) would pretty much always look like this:

- Prep new-hire paperwork
- Send new-hire paperwork (prior to starting)
- Prep incomplete paperwork
- Print incomplete paperwork (for first day)
- Sign and return paperwork
- Archive paperwork in HR system
- Share paperwork with new hire
- Receive and review signed paperwork

However, the procedure steps below a given checklist item would be different. "Prep new-hire paperwork," for example, would have varying details depending on the country, state/province, and even accessibility of the new hire (mail versus electronic). By keeping the checklist items the same, we maintain consistent SOPs while allowing for unique ways to perform the task.

Lightweight. As Atul Gawande mentioned, we need our checklists to be easy to use and not spell out everything that must be done. Checklists items are reminders, not proceduralized training. As I have helped hundreds of firms create their work checklists in Karbon over the years, I can attest that a firm owner's first instinct is to make their checklists super detailed so that not only the most junior member on the team but also any random person off the street can complete them. This is a mistake, and quickly after deployment both the firm owner and the team realize they need to remake their checklists what I call "tight and light." Even those firms that do make their checklists lightweight initially will almost always redo them every year to refine, redefine, and simplify.

To put it simply, the checklist should look and feel like a sequence of to-do notes that are written to be precise, efficient, easy to use, and easy to complete. As a user of the checklist, you should know what to do from a simple glance of an item. I recommend these principles for checklists:

- Keep item names short (like process step titles) to make them readable.

- Use verb + noun construction (like I'm doing in this list) to make them direct and actionable.

- Leave the detail to the description for fast readability and actionability.

- Use links in the description to point to detailed procedural steps (if needed) to reduce visual noise.

- Have no more than five to nine items per checklist (that are also grouped into sections) to make them feel doable.

- List only what is important to keep them efficient.

In our example, the eight steps in the paperwork sub-process are relatively tight and light. However, there could be even fewer steps and words. Remember, we want to make it quick and easy for someone to read, process, and complete. Move additional details and parameters into the item descriptions, rather than include them in the checklist item itself. Here is a quick rework to make it simpler:

- Send new-hire paperwork
- Print incomplete paperwork
- Sign paperwork
- Archive/share paperwork
- Acknowledge signed paperwork

Ownership. We'll discuss ownership and accountability in greater detail in the next chapter. For now, on a checklist we need to know who is on point for each aspect—whether it be the entire checklist (job) or a single activity within the checklist (task). If no one is responsible, nothing will get done. If two people share the responsibility, nothing will get done, since each person thinks the other will do it. Therefore, everything in and related to the checklist—whether it is the checklist item, the work status/phase, the work item itself, or even the client—must have a single owner. That ensures the client is happy, the deliverable was delivered on time, each phase was completed at quality, and not a single step was missed along the way. Here are suggestions for applying ownership to your checklists:

- One owner per item, work status, checklist, work, and client. The ownership can change between them, but there is always a single owner.

- Minimize baton passing between people. Group like-assigned checklist items together where possible.

- When the baton is passed between assignees, overcommunicate. Ensure there is no lag time between one person being done and another person picking up to own.

- Separate checklist items logically into sections—preferably by ownership (or work status). This makes the checklist item easy to mentally process and makes the checklist feel more actionable and accomplishable.

Going back to our example, it wasn't clear previously who was required to do what for each step of the process. Did you know? For the purposes of the example, I have added the owner of each step in brackets to make it clear:

- [Admin] Send new hire paperwork

- [Admin] Print incomplete paperwork

- [New Hire] Sign paperwork

- [Admin] Archive/share paperwork

- [New Hire] Acknowledge signed paperwork

Workflow. For checklist visibility and reporting, make sure the work flows logically and predictably. Typically, workflow statuses are needed for any process with more than three steps. In Jason's firm, they have a simple "tax tracker" that simply follows tax returns through the process, highlights completed returns by team member, and is checked on by a manager at least weekly during tax season. This ensures the team quickly knows what phases of the work have been completed, what phase the work is currently in, and what phase the work is headed toward.

For almost every process, the highest-level work status buckets are "planned," "ready to start," "in progress," "waiting," and "completed." Work might transition back and forth between "in progress" and "waiting." When the work has started (in progress), most knowledge-based work will follow a set sequence of work statuses that are specific to their selected industry. For example, accounting firms typically follow a work-status pattern that looks like "kick off," "prep," "process," "review," "assemble," "advise," "file," and "follow up." Some checklists or processes use all of those statuses (like tax work), while others use only a few statuses (like bookkeeping).

To ensure your work statuses provide the best trackability, visibility, and reportability, I recommend these principles:

- Define process phases as when ownership of the work changes hands or some significant amount of time exists between process steps.

- Process phases equal workflow statuses.

- Your team members must identify and relate to the work status names.

- Have no more than five to seven workflow statuses per checklist or work template.

- Less is more. Repeat workflow statuses between work templates to minimize the total number of workflow statuses you need in total.

In our previous new-hire onboarding example, I specified the work statuses as the phases that the work traversed: paperwork, proficiency, and culturalization. The phases in this case would become the work statuses for the checklist and work management system.

By converting your processes and then applying the PLOW methodology to your checklist building, you will be able to create effective, efficient, and practical checklists that will ensure all your hard work in process reinvention from Six Sigma will translate into your expected efficiency gains when your team completes their client work day in and day out. And just remember, as we discussed in the last chapter: KISS.

The Importance of Change Management

Everything we've discussed in operations management requires proper change management with the team to ensure adoption and long-term success. This is the last Six Sigma principle outlined earlier: Be flexible. While you are eager to change, your team may not be. From years of working with service organizations, I know that even the most energetic teams will always have a person or two who is reluctant. While it takes only one person to derail a great initiative, you can greatly increase your chance of success by following these change management steps to approach the change effectively—my ROADMAP to change management:

Reason: Define and communicate the "why."

Objectives: Define clear objectives, goals, strategies, and measures.

Alignment: Construct a cross-functional team that owns the "what" and "how" of the change.

Design: Define and document both the "as-is" and "to-be" processes.

Mobilize: Notify the team, execute the change, and overcommunicate the "why," "what," and "how."

Adapt: Monitor the change while holding everyone accountable. Adjust as needed.

Party: Take time to celebrate as a team when the goals are met.

Change management is critical as it enables the successful attainment of all the improvements your firm has made in TQM, Lean, Six Sigma, and checklist building. There are many methodologies you can follow; they all resemble one another. Feel free to use what you and your team prefer. If you need more details on the change management process I've outlined, visit the book's website.

Moving from Operations Management to Rhythms

Lean and Six Sigma are great operations management techniques, but they need to be modified when applied to service organizations. Why? Because they were designed for a manufacturing environment where processes are defined, results are easily measured, and machines are specific and consistent. Service organizations don't have machines. We rely on humans who are amazing *and* imperfect. Our colleagues have good days and bad days. They get sick. They go on vacation. They have life events, like having a baby, marriage, divorce, death, and vacations. People are predictably unpredictable. They simply can't deliver at Six Sigma (and almost all can't even deliver at Three Sigma: 67,000 defects per million). In respect to Lean, the eight waste categories (DOWNTIME) you want to eliminate need to be redefined to apply to a human-based production environment. Remember:

- Total Quality Management is the culture you need to cultivate.

- Lean is the mindset you need to instill.

- Six Sigma is an iterative process to create your firm's IP—your standard operating procedures.

- Checklists are your day-to-day vehicle to ensure your processes are executed flawlessly.

- Change management is essential for realizing your anticipated efficiency gains through full firm adoption.

In the next chapter, we'll look at the fourth operations management component, Rhythms (and the related reporting and metrics), which is the drivetrain that makes all this keep your organization moving forward.

10

Finding Your Organizational Rhythm

We have a scorecard with ten different metrics that every one of our employees looks at every week. The idea is to intentionally make you think about the interactions you have with your clients and your peers.

MARK SHIPTON
(INTEGRATOR OF IGNITE CPA; 24 EMPLOYEES)

S THE saying goes, you don't achieve what you don't measure. Ignite CPA, based in two offices in Alberta, Canada, is a firm that understands the importance of operations management and efficiency better than most. Focused primarily on client accounting services (payroll, bookkeeping, and accounting) in the accounting industry, Ignite CPA have quite a few technicians and bookkeepers on staff who manage high volumes of both work and communications. Even with all those client responsibilities, the firm needs its staff to have true relationships with clients to deliver on its company tagline: "Growing with you." Mark says, "We want people to be cognizant of building a relationship with clients. Winning isn't just about revenue or profit; it's also about team health."

The biggest driver of that accountability is the scorecards they put in place to measure and optimize those interactions. To ensure each and every person on the team knows their processes and their clients, they track their tasks, budgeted versus actual time for completed work, overdue item count, client interactions, quality of deliverables, email response times, and even quality and count of peer-to-peer (review) questions. That attention to detail has ensured the firm's growth, profitability, and strong retention of both clients and team. As Mark told us, "What we're looking for by tracking metrics is to generate a behavior in each individual, in whatever seat they sit in, that creates a positive outcome for our clients and team."

Getting It Rolling Smoothly

Jason Blumer

In this chapter, we dive deeply into the fourth operations management methodology mentioned in the previous chapter: Rhythms and their related reporting and metrics.

Operating mechanisms, or op mechs for short, ensure strategic alignment and operational rigor in complex organizations. Operating mechanisms provide a "rhythm" by which to manage the operations daily, weekly, monthly, quarterly, and annually, and an "engine" to ensure that a firm's strategy translates into consistent and effective execution.

There are three practical implementation considerations I'll cover to help you put operational methodologies like TQM, Lean, and Six Sigma in place and allow your service organization to run smoothly:

- Rhythms
- Reporting
- Metrics

I'll briefly define each of these, then discuss how to put them to use to ensure a firm's strategy is effectively executed. But first, we need to define some foundational mindsets that will make these three implementation considerations possible.

Ownership and Delegation

"Owner" and "ownership" are two different things. We want to be clear: The owner of the organization can't do everything (although technically they do own the business). Most service organizations were founded by a technical professional who can actually perform most of the jobs they have hired others to perform, but you can't grow while the owner still does everything, even though they possibly have the expertise to do so. So an owner must pass down *ownership* of work and tasks to other roles. If you are scaling a firm, you know this is easier said than done. But it must be done.

How do you pass down ownership? You delegate. As we'll see, for your rhythms to be successful as you grow, the ownership of the work has to have been successfully delegated. I'm highlighting this specifically because often ownership is assumed, and delegation is assumed as having happened, even though we know that humans often don't readily accept the ownership we thought we passed down. You should be making no assumptions while scaling your business. You have to empower your teams to take the reins, and you must be ultra clear in your communication of who owns the work and when delegation has happened (because reverse delegation, where the team gives you work back to finish, dismantles growth). In the example that started this chapter, Ignite CPA makes ownership obvious and accountable by handing down the maintenance of scorecards to its team.

To clarify, here's the equation: Delegation + Ownership = Empowering a team to lead and be successful.

At a high level, here are the six components of delegation:

- Trust: Delegate with risk of failure.

- Clarity and alignment: Set clear goals, objectives, roles, and timing.

- Ownership: Clearly select and state who's who in the zoo (e.g., DACI and RASCI, which we'll discuss next).

- Cadence: Ensure the rhythm and reason of meetings with a visible scoreboard.

- Communication: Reinforce constant and constructive feedback. Use a tech tool to lower the barriers.

- Support: Outline who is available and how they can help.

DACI and RASCI

We can use some mental models to make sure that delegation is happening swiftly, with the right communication, and that ownership has finally found its place on the right team member's plate. The DACI model was developed by Intuit to support decision making:

Driver: The person who drives the decision—the "owner"

Approver: The person who makes the decision

Contributor(s): The person/people providing input or whose knowledge helps the work to be done effectively

Informed: The person/people who might be affected or who need to be kept informed by the delegation

A similar but expanded model is RASCI:

Responsible: The person responsible for the entire project/work

Accountable: The person with ultimate control over the success of the work

Supportive: The person/people who provide support and assistance to the responsible and accountable team members

Consulted: The valuable subject matter experts who can provide knowledge and input to those responsible

Informed: The person/people who might be affected or who need to be kept informed by the delegation

With these models in place, think through the roles in your firm, who embodies these roles, and how you can bring clarity to the roles you've hired to get the work done while you scale. For a growing, large organization with structure, the underlying team members must have a defined structure of ownership, and it must be clear when delegation has taken place. Any time two people own something, nothing gets done. The same is obviously true if no one owns the work. In addition, those who approve and decide must be pre-defined. And as you grow, we can never underestimate how important it is to communicate, communicate, communicate these concepts of ownership and delegation so that your rhythms remain effective on an ongoing basis.

Delegation plus ownership takes work, planning, and follow-up. Some members of your team may call this micromanaging, but don't accept that label (unless in fact you are micromanaging). Remind them that it is prudent to assign, define, inform, and follow up on what has been delegated so that no assumptions are being made around ownership. What is often at the heart of push-back and labels like "micromanagement" is that people just want to be left alone to do things the way they want to do them. We all feel that way at times. Our team has felt that before, and what they are really pushing against is how the scaffolding of structure is surrounding them in tighter ways. Are we doing that to strangle them? Of course not, but a team can feel a tightening as you add structure around ownership and delegation. We've been accused of micromanaging when what we were doing was requiring things from our team that they didn't want us to require. So now we always try to counter the "tightening of structure" with communication of what is coming with this new structure and why we believe it is strategic to add it.

And if you *are* micromanaging, stop it.

MICROMANAGING

This is an inappropriate oversight on the smallest details of a team member's work. Instead of focusing on the outcomes, the micromanager often forces work and work environments to be constructed their way without regard for the outcome. The micromanager refuses to give up ownership, makes nitpicky corrections that don't matter for the outcome to be delivered, and maintains decision making (or trumps previously made decisions without telling anyone) even after voicing that ownership has been passed down to someone else.

With ownership and delegation defined, let's dive into our three op mechs: rhythms, reporting, and metrics.

Rhythms

As we have said repeatedly, you are operating a human organization. Humans need far more grace than machines in how they work, yet they also need accountability to remain focused on their work output.

In service organizations, we wrap rhythms around the humans that work in our organizations. What do we wrap them with? A calendar. In service organizations that are seeking to grow, the calendar is an underused tool. It is the perfect representation of the thing every human has available to them: We all get 24/7/365. Warren Buffett and I both have access to the same real estate on the calendar. The calendar levels the playing field and creates clarity as teams collaborate to produce and give service to the markets they serve. Op mechs run on calendars in service firms—when we say rhythms, we mean calendar rhythms. A calendar rhythm is putting a block on your calendar with these three important guiding aspects:

- On the same day
- At the same time
- On the recurrence of the rhythm

For example, instead of saying, "Our team needs to meet each week to review this process," and then everyone tries to find a time to meet, we instead schedule a process review meeting to happen every month, on the third Tuesday, at 9 am EST. You can block this on a calendar, invite the people involved, and make it recur on the same day, at the same time, and on the defined recurrence.

A rhythm is planned in advance, everyone is informed and can give feedback on its timing, and then everyone accepts it. It becomes habitual for the people involved, and this is where the power lies. When something is habitual, it becomes predictable, and predictable things sink down into a team's working processes so they become second nature. Once a rhythm is set, people just habitually show up. No fighting, no questions, and no other things getting in the way. Once seated, a rhythm is a superpower in the operational side of a scaling service organization. So instead of the chaos of trying to set a meeting with a team, the rhythm guides the participation.

The pandemic certainly made adherence to rhythms more necessary than ever. Previously, firms were made up of people in the same location, working the same hours, and culturally on the "same page" because they were in the same office. Meetings could be more ad hoc—created when needed—since everyone was in the same location. If you recall from the Practice Excellence survey employment statistics outlined in Chapter 7, we see firms desperately seeking competent staff in any way possible and moving beyond full-time employment to employing staff in various other ways simultaneously, such as part-time employees, outsourced resources, and fractional, seasonal, and gig workers.

Several years past the infamous year 2020, we know our work will never "go back to the way it was." For example, we see in the Practice Excellence survey that over 30 percent of firms are now made up of employees who work outside of the office (and many outside the firm's country of origin). This isn't just within a given employee size segment; it exists in firms of every size. Having meetings at a set time is so much more critical, since it is more difficult to ensure all team levels are on task and aligned. It is harder to keep a pulse on things as a firm owner today, but rhythms will allow you to do this, since the calendar carries an organization through its operations.

Further, deploying rhythms into your team takes some weight off the operational department and team members who may be tasked with setting ongoing meetings, finding times people can get together, or figuring out a time for a meeting to review a particular process. Instead of trying to find an ad hoc time to meet to review a process, service organizations become much more valuable when they set a rhythm to review various processes on a set day and time and recurring in a particular pattern.

There is a "height" to our rhythms as well, called the altitude. The altitude of the meeting rhythm speaks to whether it is organizationally focused, focused on the work, focused on the team, et cetera. The altitude will also help you define who leads the rhythm and who comes to it. Let's bring back our Service Organizational Strata from Chapter 3 and lay out the layers of altitude so you can see examples of how to employ rhythms in your organization at the right altitude.

Service Organizational Strata Rhythms and Ownership

Service Org Stratum	Daily <15 to 30 minutes	Weekly 30 minutes	Monthly 60 minutes	Quarterly 60 to 90 minutes	Annually 90 minutes
Flat: solo to 7	Team	Org owner	Org owner	Org owner	Org owner
Management: 8 to 12	Technical team lead	Management	Management/ Org owner	Org owner	Org owner
Departmental: 13 to 25	Technical team lead/ Department leads	Management/ Department leads	Management/ Department leads	Leadership	Org owner
Leadership: 26 to 50	Technical team lead	Technical team lead	Management/ Department leads	Leadership	Org owner

First, notice the table shows us higher-frequency rhythms on the left-hand side than on the right-hand side (moving from daily to annually). Second, you'll see team and team leads more on the left-hand side of the table (where the frequencies of rhythms are higher), and you'll see managers and owners on the right-hand side of the table (where the frequencies are lower in volume). The *altitude* of the rhythms becomes higher as you move from left to right in the table—in other words, owners tend to stay in the rhythms on the right-hand side.

Typically, your low-level, high-frequency (daily, weekly) meetings are primarily managed bottom-up by employees or team leads (at a low altitude). The phrase "low-level" is not a value statement about an employee; it means rhythms that are closest to the delivery of the work and the client. Another name for this can be "tactical." On the other hand, your high-level, low-frequency (monthly, quarterly) meetings are driven from the top down (at a higher altitude). The phrase "high-level" here references organization-focused rhythms, as opposed to the tactical work of revenue generation. Another name for this can be "strategic."

TACTICAL

Closest to the work, high frequency, and at a low altitude.

STRATEGIC

Closest to the organization, low frequency, and at a high altitude.

Low-level meetings are often individual report outs (i.e., stand-ups) and reflections of task completion and task planning (look backs, plan forwards, and weekly catch-ups), while high-level meetings are organizational/departmental level report outs on a monthly and quarterly basis (project recap/projections/new team introductions/firm-wide review/role updates). Annual rhythms in the far right column in the table become reserved for relaying the value of the organization, financial reporting, vision, structural changes, and new departments or service line introductions.

Notice in the table that as the organization grows larger, the owners are handing down rhythms to other people. By this we mean that owners will exit rhythms found on the left-hand side of the table first, and they continue to do so as they move to the right of the table. This is handing down the altitude of the rhythm to another leader as they grow in the organization. As a team is promoted, they can also be given rhythms to lead as the owner exits the ownership of those rhythms. So as you promote a leader, you don't give them more revenue-generating work; you delegate rhythms for them to lead for the organization. This essentially promotes the right team member higher into the altitudes of the rhythms that make the organization work in a sustainable way. As an owner, as you hand down a rhythm to a promoted team member, you will also teach them how to lead within that rhythm.

Look at the table layers horizontally now. The need for a higher frequency of rhythms grows as the organization itself grows larger. In the solo to 7-team-member stratum, there may not need to be many rhythms, and the owner is leading most of them. Yet in a larger organization, there is more complexity to manage, so the rhythms are built strategically to cull chaos as the organization expands through its complexity. In the 26- to 50-team-member stratum, you'll see many different types of roles embedded in the rhythms. This table shows that rhythms become more frequent to support the bulkiness of the service organization in its structure and scaffolding.

Here we'll remind you of what we told you in one of the first chapters: If you want to lead a better organization, you must intentionally design the organization to operate more efficiently and effectively. Installing rhythms at the appropriate altitudes is your job as the leader, and it will cull the chaos of your service organization as you scale larger.

Reporting

Reporting is the second essential. Many consultancies, agencies, firms, and other service organizations run too much information in their minds. The mind is not the place to keep important data, especially data that you are meant to make sense of on any regular rhythm. Reporting is for everyone, from the owners to the last team member, and is at the heart of how you measure your organization's progress.

As we saw in the story of Ignite CPA at the beginning of this chapter, scorecards are a great example of reporting that produces the measurement needed for an organization to track its growth.

What's more, a service organization needs to produce more complex reporting as the organization becomes more complex. We've highlighted several times already that the complexity of scaling an organization requires the founder/owner to respond to manage that complexity effectively. As you grow, you'll add more measurement through your expanded efforts of reporting.

At a minimum, as you head toward eight people on your service organization's team, you need to respond with regular reporting to accumulate the information somewhere other than your own mind so you can make sense of it. There are many types of data you would report on, but we suggest these three important guiding buckets of data:

- Clients/revenue

- Team/capacity

- Finance/profitability

Note that these suggested measurements reference the 3 Rs Framework, with the fourth R (results) thrown in related to profitability. Here they are as a reminder:

The 3 Rs of Reporting

The Organization's Profit & Loss Components	The 3 Rs Framework	Reporting on Buckets of Data
Revenue	Revenue	Clients/Revenue
Expense team following accountable processes	Resources & Recipes	Team/ Capacity
Profit	Results	Financial/ Profitability

Inherent in the need for reporting is the need to keep your technical (accounting, engineering, design, etc.), operations, and team structures updated. With updated systems comes regular reporting. We've met small service-organization founders who just ignore their data (like their monthly bookkeeping) because they get so busy. As they grow, they become unable to produce the reporting they need to run their organization. You can't manage what you don't measure and report on. As you grow, you may be sorry you didn't invest in regular reporting when your organization was smaller in size, because it gets harder to add in reporting for a more complex organization after it's grown larger.

Traditionally, many service organizations tracked profitability through lenses that have become old and archaic. They may report on the following:

- Financials: Revenue, profitability, and income per owner

- Cash flow: AR management, WIP management, lock up (days)

- Clients: Year-over-year client growth

- Staffing: Average staff compensation, attrition rate, staff-to-partner ratio

- Productivity: Utilization and realization

Not all these measurements provide poor information, but there may be more we need to report on that better reflects how the service industry is changing with the market it serves. And it has definitely changed post-pandemic in ways that we believe it will never go back to. We may need new reporting due to these factors:

- Cadence of service: Instead of once a year or project revenue, we are seeing more recurring and subscription-based services. Further, the markets we serve are becoming more familiar with this and are even allowing us to draft our revenue from their bank accounts, rather than invoicing for it.

- Type of revenue: Compliance versus advisory means we are selling higher levels of advice (or opinions), which requires a different level of focus for a team member and one client (as opposed to one team member serving large groups of clients). The implementation and fast adoption of AI is further supporting this move away from tactical types of revenue to more advisory revenue.

- Staffing: Working virtually rather than in the office could mean the levels of revenue the team can handle may be changing due to the higher level of distractions, a younger workforce with new requirements for work, and different forms of communication.

- Communication: Virtual teams operate in an asynchronous way, where there is a "communicate and wait" mentality, as opposed to synchronous work in the same location, where the knowledge could be disseminated back and forth concurrently in the moment.

- Departmentalization: As firms grow, a hierarchical organizational design is required, resulting in a more complex business structure. For both teams and individuals to monitor their progress, this increasingly complex structure requires more formalized reporting.

- Technology: AI is moving our technology toward containing its own knowledge and providing that knowledge to us, as opposed to us getting our input from research and compiling our own information, which is decidedly slower. This should lead to more efficient service and higher revenue reporting per team member.

- Clients: Relationship-driven rather than transactional approaches mean service organizations are switching to fewer client relationships with higher price tags due to the focus and attention clients are willing to pay for.

- Time horizon: Reactive (lag) versus proactive (lead) also supports the fact that service relationships with clients are expanding and contracts may be one or two years in length as opposed to just seasons that extend the length of a project or a transactional service. Now contracts can extend the length of a relationship. With longer timelines, we are no longer selling services but rather relationships (which are more valuable).

With changes in our world and how we serve, we must learn to abandon old ways of measurement and reporting and adopt new ways that reflect the reporting we actually need in our scaling service organizations.

Metrics

Metrics are really a subset of reporting. Data must be accumulated in compact forms so owners can make quick decisions from the insights. Reporting is *all* of the data, while metrics are only meant to be a summary of the most important data. Reporting is everything you can know about your firm, while metrics are summaries of that information, usually presented on a rhythmic basis in some form of calculation or numeric summation of a larger data set. You can call them KPIs, OKRs, measurements, et cetera. Eventually, owners hand down reporting duties to other team members (in low-altitude rhythms), while the executives and owners receive the metrics in summary form presented to them, allowing them to quickly make decisions on the information that is the most important.

Metrics can rarely depict reality in just one set of data in one moment in time. Metrics don't provide too much in the way of insight if they show just one moment. Metrics make more sense presented consistently over a period, so that the pattern of the metric is what produces the insights.

As an example, new leaders in your organization can research metrics for one point in time or a difficult situation they are trying to understand with another team member they lead. From this research, they can "mistake coincidence for conspiracy" as to what that metric is teaching the leaders. They may think the team member they lead is performing poorly, when it may only show a point in time during a difficult week for the team member. A hyperfocus on a point in time will often lead to wrong conclusions when leveraging metrics. We want patterns of the metric, over time, through seasons of our firm's life and through the ups and downs of our team's lives. When we stop believing phantom patterns in the data, then a genuine picture can emerge over time.

As we mentioned, the world is changing and so must our metrics. For example, let's look at the popular revenue/FTE metric. This is where revenue for the company is divided by some average of a full-time equivalent (FTE). This metric was meant to consider that there are some revenue-generating team members and some non-revenue-generating team members in a services company, and we needed to determine if they were all producing the right amount of revenue, *on average*. It is an effective metric, and we have a lot of benchmarks to compare our revenue to using this metric. However, as service organizations change to be able to service fewer clients at higher prices, we are seeing an advisory shift in the types of services we offer and the types of advisory departments we create. (AI is one of our newest "team members" and will further aid us in this shift.)

This shift leads us to be able to assign revenue to one person in a firm (where that one person may hold the service of a small group of clients). With this assignment comes the ability to track a new metric, revenue per person (RPP). Revenue/FTE was a "summarized" metric (and still good), while RPP is a more specific metric for a revenue-generating team member. It allows us to see the specific team members and exactly how much revenue they are assigned (e.g., $150,000 per revenue-generating person). Further, RPP also allows us to see which team members should *not* produce revenue (operations, director-level team, etc.) or what percent of their time should be devoted to revenue and what percent to the service of the

Only the guy who isn't rowing has time to rock the boat.

ATTRIBUTED TO JEAN-PAUL SARTRE

organization. We've seen this breakdown depicted visually in the Team Structure Capacity Chart conversation from Chapter 6. Now, with the RPP, we can specifically discuss how to best leverage each person's employment for the good of the organization.

There are many forms of metrics you will want to track. For our purposes, we suggest metrics produce these three important guiding types of data to compare:

- Trending comparisons

- Actual versus anticipated comparisons

- Time-based comparisons

Again, these are *types* of metrics. Your specific metrics will sit within these broader metric types.

Trending comparisons involves comparing one set of data to similar sets. If you show metrics for May, you should also show the same metrics for January through April. Looking at the data side by side from January to May produces trends and creates a more informed consumer of the metric data.

Actual versus anticipated comparisons are similar to actual versus budget financial data. There is a lot to learn by predicting or anticipating what you want a certain metric to look like (the budget) and then comparing what that data set came out to be (the actual). Your prediction of that metric becomes more accurate and sophisticated over time as you seek to compare the anticipated budget metric to the actual data produced by the reporting.

Time-based comparisons are the third important way to summarize and display metrics out of a large data set of reports. If you show a current period, show the month-to-date and year-to-date as well. The current month's metric will make more sense within the context of the same metric also reported on a quarterly and annual basis. A current month metric bumped up against an annual metric can show you if the current month is an anomaly, some form of seasonality that you can expect each year during that same time, or a significant change in a trend you now need to accommodate for.

The principle of metrics in our firm that we reiterate to our team is to never show one set of data in a column by itself; "Data should never be alone," we like to say. Data sets must always be presented beside other data sets. Further, metrics are always being tweaked and changed. You won't get to a final set of metrics because your organization will always be growing in complexity, thus changing in the type of data that you need to lead your organization.

Putting It All Together

Let's develop a table that will lead us in the operations management techniques we need using the methodologies in the previous and the current chapter. In the Rhythmic Reporting Examples table, you'll see the suggested rhythms for each type of operations management mechanism we suggest as you scale your service organization. This is not a full chart for you to use but simply an example you will build from for your own service firm, agency, or other service organization. You can use this chart below and the one earlier in this chapter on service organizational strata rhythms.

Rhythmic Reporting Examples

Type of Rhythm	Rhythm Recurrence	Reporting/ Metrics	Stated Purpose
Partner/ Owner	First week of November, 9 am to 4 pm EST, annually	Strategic initiatives, documenting initiatives	Annual strategic planning to decide goals for 1 and 3 years out
Partner/ Owner	Mon and Fri, 10 am to 12 pm EST, weekly	Goals complete/ incomplete, review of leadership team data and metrics	Growth planning, decision making, 90-day goal reviews for company, data and reporting to push down to team
Leadership team	Wed, 10 am EST, weekly	Goals complete/ incomplete, company financial revenue and profitability metric summary reviews, review of team capacity allocation and revenue produced by team member, per client	Decision making, 90-day goal reviews for company
Senior team	Tue, 10 am EST, weekly	Project management review of % of workflow tasks complete/ incomplete, tracking of overall team struggles, high-level review of client issues/ barriers to service	Support technical team, review technical team progress, move service forward, identify struggling team and reasons why

Rhythmic Reporting Examples

Type of Rhythm	Rhythm Recurrence	Reporting/ Metrics	Stated Purpose
Project/ Account management	Mon and Fri huddles, 9 am EST, weekly	Review of task dashboard for team member, service struggle areas, calendar review	Move particular service forward for particular clients, identify struggling team and reasons why
Technical	1st and 3rd Mon, 10 am EST, monthly	Leadership team educational initiatives, dashboard of all team completions/ non-completions of work	Technical education, service announcements, discuss firm service methodologies, and tackle technical service issues that affect team
Cultural	Wed, 12 pm EST, weekly	Core value countdown/ call outs	Cultural adherence
Client service	Recurrences set with each client	Client financial and technical reporting and overall work movement	Particular client service

As I said at the beginning of this chapter, our goal is to tie our strategy to our execution. Our rhythms, reporting, and metrics help us do this. They are the bridge between the two, or the "engine" to operate your organization.

There are a number of things to note about our Rhythmic Reporting Examples table. First, everything trickles down from a strategic vantage point. As with the first table in this chapter, the strategy of growth at the top informs all layers of the rhythms below the strategy. The most strategic behaviors are at the top of the rhythmic chart and involve the owners who make these decisions—which is to say, the altitude of the rhythms is highest at the top and lowest at the bottom of the table. Even the order of the day of the rhythmic meetings matters so that growth strategy is directing the context of annual and multi-year growth into each week's leadership, technical, and cultural meetings. In the second column of the table, you'll notice that partner/owner rhythms come first in the week (Monday), followed by leadership rhythms, then followed by team rhythms. This is not exact, but it does inform how strategy flows down to inform all other functions of the organization's operations. As teams work and make decisions and serve clients each week, having the context of growth passed down from a strategic higher altitude level can better inform those lower-altitude decisions.

We've mentioned this point earlier in the chapter, but it bears repeating. As we move down the rhythmic reporting table, owners are meant to exit lower-level rhythms so they remain in high-level strategic areas of the company. When you as the owner promote someone, it means you may get to exit a rhythm you were previously in and have the promoted team member fulfill that rhythm now. This way, even as the service organization grows, the same owners can manage a growing team, increasing revenue, and an increasingly complex organization. Leaders, seniors, and the technical team are meant to operate and fulfill the revenue with concurrent capacity. In the lower levels of the rhythmic reporting table, you'll see that the focus is on service, team care, client care, and eliminating barriers to the efficient production of revenue.

Another point to reinforce: Because the owners remain in the upper levels of the rhythmic reporting table, they are meant to receive more summarized data from the leaders, seniors, and technical team on a regular basis. The owners do not manage or review the full data set of reporting (e.g., reviewing every team member's to-do list in the project management system each week) but instead teach the leaders and seniors how to produce summarized metrics that effectively provide the necessary information so the owners

You can't manage what you don't measure.

ATTRIBUTED TO PETER DRUCKER

can continue making accurate and timely decisions related to growth. So data is more summarized in the higher altitude. As you move down the table, you can give larger sets of reporting data to more specialized teams and roles that are focused on more narrow rhythms.

Lastly, owners should not skip down to rhythms they have set other teams to lead and report on. Owners and partners lead *through* the other layers and should try not to "go around" the layers they have set in place. This is where leverage of leadership teams comes into play and allows the same set of owners to manage and grow an increasingly complex organization. Leadership leverage is the art of leading from one to many.

However, although the owners do not skip down rhythmic levels, they can lead particularly by exception. This means there are exceptions the owners can employ in order to get more involved in the granular workings of the firm—*but only by exception*. This may happen when there is a high-risk issue with a team member or client that is urgent or cannot effectively be managed by the leaders and seniors of the organization in a timely way. At this point, an owner may take over a decision, a meeting, a service issue, or team leadership, and then only temporarily, to quickly mitigate the high risk to the organization. If this happens, it will be important for the leader to again exit that lower rhythm after the emergency is averted and move to the higher altitude rhythms embodied in their role.

Rhythms aren't just for meetings. You can use a rhythm to cull the chaos in any part of your business. For example, as a service organization offers more and more complicated revenue service to their market, they can consider narrowing the service rhythms with the client from monthly to weekly. This more complicated revenue is often called consultative or advisory work. Such work has higher levels of unknowns and thus more troubled areas in client service. To offset this risk, a more tightly defined rhythm (e.g., from monthly to weekly) can mitigate the risk that is inherent in the amount of knowledge being managed for clients in advisory work.

As another example, if a team member is struggling with their work fulfillment and lacks an understanding of their role, you can apply a tighter rhythm of care so that project management huddles happen weekly on Mondays and Fridays, as opposed to just monthly for all other team members. This allows for the correction and support of the team member's struggle over a shorter period of time, minimizing the risk of the loss of revenue fulfillment with the client.

As you look at your business and note areas where a rhythm may be needed, assess what data you have to report on and then develop a metric that can be prepared to produce trending and comparisons to make use of in that rhythmic meeting you've put on the calendar. Let's work through an example of how to build a trending rhythm you need to install in your organization.

- Area in your organization where you need a rhythm: Second review on advisory reporting for a client on a monthly basis. Issue: You've noticed that advisory reports keep getting to the clients with incorrect data and the second review is not catching these errors.

- Set the rhythm with a practical service-level protocol: "All accounting for clients is completed by the twelfth of each month, and second reviews by the manager are due by the twentieth of each month."

- The senior project lead reports on two new metrics each month:
  - Days lagging from accounting close—how many days after the twelfth was each client's accounting records closed?
  - Days lagging from second review—how many days after the twentieth were each client's accounting records reviewed by a manager?

- The client services manager tracks the trending of all "days lagging…" for the accounting close each month and the second review each month.

- In the leadership team weekly meeting rhythm, the client services manager reports to the owners the trend of year-to-date, quarter-to-date, and current month of "days lagging…" for accounting and second reviews. Analysis: The trends are analyzed for patterns of disruption by team member, poor design of the service-level protocol, season of the year, et cetera.

Note that you can design any set of reported data to be turned into any metric you need, as well as reported on any rhythm you choose. You are the designer of your organization! As you consider the concepts in this chapter, make sure to remain open and creative as to how these concepts could apply to your service firm. Fight the desire to simply copy what we've developed here and instead seek to apply the principles to your own intimate model of service, the issues you have, and the team you leverage to serve your particular clients. To combat the variability of scaling and increasing your firm's profitability, what you are striving for is incremental process improvement, increased process efficiency (through decreased waste), and, ultimately, higher customer satisfaction and employee engagement, ensuring the continued value of the enterprise you are building.

Next, we're going to make you a master of planning and make sure you consider future revenue changes, how to balance that with your team's capacity commitments, and the uncertainty of time. Buckle up!

11

Planning Across Multiple Horizons

Driven by a passion for innovation and a desire
to create a more personalized client experience, I shifted
away from traditional tax and audit services
toward one-on-one personalized advisory work.

GARY WOOD, CPA
(OWNER OF CRC; 12 EMPLOYEES)

N THE beautiful Ozarks in Missouri, Gary Wood took over
ownership of a traditional, tax-only-focused CPA firm over ten
years ago. Gary is a family man, has four kids, and is community-
minded and focused on improving the lives and businesses in his
local area. He cares deeply about his clients, his employees, and his
family, and he isn't concerned about firm growth as much as he is
about employee burnout. He is innovative in an industry that isn't
considered for it, and he has a passion for breaking the mold while
creating new molds for old ways of doing things. So, in owning the
firm, he was seeking out how to best plan for the future to ensure the
needs of the firm didn't negatively affect the lives of his employees
and his family:

When Kevin [Yount] and I took over the firm, we immediately set out to break the mold of the century-old dysfunction in CPA firms: cramming 80 percent of their annual revenues into 20 percent of their annual capacity. How can you achieve effective capacity planning and deliver excellent client service within this broken model?

With intentional scaling, we design our organizational systems intimately for our companies, not letting tradition dictate that we use old, broken models. For Gary, the old model created sleepless nights worrying about pairing supply with demand. The old firm staffed for fifty-two weeks, hoping enough demand, production, and profit would come through in a ten-week busy season to make it all worth it! So, Gary created a new mold. As tax-only firms are highly seasonal and typically bill after the fact, Gary needed to remove the uncertainty and compressed nature of his demand by growing the relationships of his clients from being once a year to ongoing throughout the year. By smoothing out his demand, he could maintain a reasonable work schedule for his employees and not have to deal with seasonal hiring or requiring his team to work overtime during tax season. To tackle these difficulties, Gary and his team developed three standardized seasons. This framework, which CRC proudly calls their Three Seasons Framework, involves multiple collaborative meetings with clients throughout the year for reviews, planning, and updates. This was the critical unlock: creating demand for year-round service to finally align with their year-round supply (capacity) by productizing their service schedule. Gary highlights, "The legacy firm had thousands of clients paying a few hundred bucks a year, but now we have a few hundred clients paying thousands of dollars a year."

To further reduce complexity, and as part of his "lifestyle firm" culture, Gary intentionally aims for year-over-year flat revenue while allowing for "accidental growth." To accomplish this, Gary softened his constraints by fixing the up-front yearly engagements to 70 percent of his capacity and left 30 percent capacity free to accept new clients throughout the year. Since taking over ownership, Gary, after ten years, has transitioned the business to be 30 percent tax compliance and 70 percent advisory, with all clients on subscription billing. And today, he has a backlog of potential clients that want to work with CRC, plus he has clients, employees, and a family that love both him and his firm. As he says:

> We're in an environment with more work than people. This means we get to choose. It's no longer about, "How many hours do I have to work?" It's now about, "How many hours do I want to work, and what client base allows me to earn what I need while working those hours?" It's about taking control.

Time to Plan?

Ian Vacin

Let's take a step back from where we have been in the last few chapters. In Chapter 8, we discussed the two nemeses of capacity planning, variability and uncertainty, and our constant pursuit of minimizing their impact so we can drive optimal profitability and success for our service organizations. For the past few chapters, we have discussed operations management at length to combat variability. Now we want to look at uncertainty in greater depth. Remember that the key factors influencing both nemeses from Chapter 8 were the aspects of past (history), present (firm complexity), and future (time). As we focus on uncertainty in a deeper way, we'll see that time is the biggest aspect to account for and the biggest hurdle to overcome. So, let's dig deeper into time—not time tracking, but rather the vector and consideration of time: the seconds, minutes, hours, days, and months that tick past us all, no matter what we do.

As we learned previously, everything centers on our understanding of capacity. You have to tackle questions like these (and many more):

- How many people do you have?

- What roles can they play?

- How much time are they promising to the business?

- How productive are they now?

- How much of that time can be assigned to client/billable work?

Capacity combined with time now adds a whole additional level of complexity, especially when we focus on our resources. Who you have today isn't necessarily who you will have tomorrow. Some people quit. Some people are fired (or should be). Some people go on leave. Some never come back. Some go part-time. Some want to do more than their typical workload (for more money or recognition). Some work harder and are more productive. Some become lazy and become less productive. But how do you know? When will these things happen? The answer is always: In time.

In our one-hundred-plus interviews, firm owner after firm owner expressed their concern about the disruption when a productive member on the team becomes unavailable and how some team members seem to be less productive ("more lazy") over time. This is on top of the overarching concern that they currently feel they don't have enough staff or are behind on hiring the next staff member. They know in their gut that they are in trouble, but they don't know exactly why and by how much.

Do you feel that? Time is part of the problem. Access to good data, understanding your planning horizons (more on that in a moment), and building a plan that handles today, tomorrow, next month, this quarter, next quarter, and this year will remove that anxiety. Another part of the problem is making time to do the planning. In our quantitative survey, only 51 percent did capacity planning and almost 10 percent didn't do any of the planning activities outlined in this chapter. As the old proverb says, "Failing to plan is planning to fail." Let's learn to plan like Gary Wood did.

PLANNING HORIZON

Planning horizons are different ranges in time (e.g., daily, weekly, monthly, quarterly, annually) that support different planning methods (e.g., work prioritization, load balancing, etc.) to provide the right information at the right visibility to make proper planning decisions at the right altitude.

A Wrinkle in Time

In time, as in space, the closer things are, the more clearly you can see them. The uncertainty that time creates is represented as increased variability in your capacity and planning models as you look out into the future.

When we built our MELT model of capacity discounting and tracking in Chapter 6, we had near-perfect information. We knew the time commitments of our team for this week, this month, and most likely this quarter. We knew upcoming team vacations, company holidays, and other time-off events that reduced the overall time commitment per week per team member. If we implemented the learning from the previous chapters, then we knew what role(s) each person can perform and what clients they are or will be working with. Further, many owners of service organizations have weekly or monthly one-on-ones and use HR tools to measure employee sentiment. Thus, they have a sense of the emotional headspace of their employees and are able to adjust each staff member's productivity based on their MELT. As a result, you can create a solid capacity plan for the immediate future—which we define as this upcoming quarter.

Even with that, we've still got a problem. You need to plan even longer than that. Be like Gary and have the next year planned out and fully understood. However, it always seems that after the plan is completed and we begin to execute it, the unexpected always happens—a person quits, a big client leaves, or a process fails. Unfortunately, a capacity plan requires all its parameters, minus the MELT, to be fixed. But is it really possible to do that? For example, do your employees know when they will be on vacation next quarter or even in the next year? Can your employees let you know when they plan to go on leave for a personal event (like a funeral) and how long that leave will be? Will your employees tell you when they plan to quit beyond the two weeks' courtesy notice they typically give? No, they don't know, and they wouldn't tell you if they did. For capacity planning in future quarters, you have imperfect information. So how do you manage this issue of uncertainty, specifically in regard to capacity planning?

Let's bring back our advice from capacity complexities: Keep it simple, stupid.

Remember what Gary did? He simplified things by constraining one of his variables (human resources) to enable him to calculate the revenue for his annual plan. Similarly, as you build your capacity planning for future quarters, just simplify your parameters from MELT to just T, where time is the only thing that is important. It all comes down to time promised by your team members (e.g., forty hours per week) minus their expected time off (straight-lined amount for their annual paid time-off allotment and sick leave), and then adjusted down by the steady-state productivity they have demonstrated in the past quarter or year for the role they play on the team (individual contributor, manager, leader, etc.). If you want to be more conservative, you can add a further buffer by reducing your human capacity by 5 percent based on your risk tolerance, and you can also model that in your planning methods, which we'll discuss later.

By making the modeling of your future capacity simple for time periods outside of the upcoming quarter, the variability of time and the law of large numbers will work together to get you close enough to provide the necessary inputs for your other long-term planning activities. Don't overthink it. Just make it happen. Get to your future period capacity planning using simple numbers, and avoid your desire to be "accurate" as you move further out into the future.

Now, when simplifying capacity in future periods like this, we didn't create a capacity plan, we created a workforce plan. Let's take a step back and look across time at the various planning methods that firms use successfully to make the best decisions based on the various planning horizons. Our upcoming matrices will help to bring these concepts and ideas together for you.

What's on the Horizon?

In business, there are discrete time periods that are simply stated as short-term, medium-term, and long-term. For most firms, those discrete time periods correspond to the planning time horizons of today, this week, this month, this quarter, next quarter, this year, and beyond. As we move from today to this year, things become less defined, more variable, and more complicated. This is where uncertainty creeps in.

As we look across the time horizons, what is really shifting and changing? We'll highlight this with our Time Horizon Planning Matrix tables (shown later), which will define and detail our planning variables and planning attributes. From these matrix tables, we'll show how the variables and attributes of planning influence the various planning methods (aka planning tools) that we'll need in order to manage the changing landscape over time. Before we look at the tables, let's define the seven different planning methods:

- Work prioritization
- Load balancing
- Production planning
- Capacity planning
- Workforce planning
- Annual planning
- Horizon planning

Work Prioritization

(real-time planning; reviewed daily;
83 percent of firms implement)

The What and How: Owned by each individual contributor, work prioritization ensures that an individual's to-dos and checklist items are ranked and prioritized based on their importance and urgency to achieve the goals set by themselves and the team over a given week. Remember in previous chapters we discussed prioritization as a concept and how important, and difficult, the concept is for service professionals to engage in.

Note: Because everything is fixed, inflexible, and known, if the work can't be completed on time, there are typically few options available except to deliver the work to the client late or below quality, to shoulder tap a colleague for assistance, or for someone to work overtime to complete it.

Load Balancing

(near-term planning; reviewed weekly;
62 percent of firms implement)

The What: Looking across their team, team leads will review the collective work over the coming weeks (typically this month) and redistribute the workload evenly across their team members to prevent bottlenecks and overtime. This ultimately feeds into the work prioritization that individuals on the team are managing themselves.

The How: Most often, team leads will review the number of jobs on each person's plate and rebalance evenly across the team members, as the work and team members are typically similar. This is where it is advantageous to build service delivery pods (as mentioned in Chapter 4). However, the rebalancing between team members might not be "even," as the team leads must factor in individual team member productivity levels and client relationship priorities. When the work is not similar, the team leads might look at a different metric to balance from—typically the amount of revenue owned by each team member (calculated and tracked by the revenue per person metric in the previous chapter).

Note: If the work system is overloaded, the same negative outcomes in work prioritization would exist here. However, the impact would typically be less severe, as the issues would be addressed earlier in time and could be spread across a higher number of employees.

Production Planning
(short-term planning; reviewed monthly;
52 percent of firms implement)

The What: Owned by the team managers (and supported by the operations manager, or a similar high-level oversight role), production planning takes the demand and resources available for the given period (e.g., upcoming quarter) to create a detailed roadmap (typically represented as a visual Gantt chart) specifying when work is to be started and completed and by whom. The production plan uses the capacity plan as an input (where both supply and demand are now fixed) and seeks to ensure the right resources are available and allocated appropriately to meet the associated work deadlines, while minimizing bottlenecks and waste (typically represented by high-skilled labor performing lower-level work).

The How: Because things inevitably don't go to plan, the production plan is reviewed monthly and readjusted to best enable the organization to meet client project deadlines while maximizing firm profitability. Unlike work prioritization and load balancing, there is a bit more flexibility to work with. Since the capacity plan fixes both demand and resources, role-based bottlenecks become visible when completing the production plan due to the sequencing of work. While there is a small possibility of plugging that gap through hiring, typically gaps are resolved by using high-skilled staff (e.g., utility players), expanding resource availability (e.g., overtime), or stealing time from non-billable activities—all of which cut into firm profitability.

Note: The production plan is one of the most complicated planning methods to complete in service organizations because employees have differing roles and skills and the project work typically requires multiple people, some technical and some not technical, to complete it. As mentioned in Chapter 7, your utility players are infinitely valuable when performing production planning, as they can easily fill the gaps and issues that emerge when creating this complicated and detailed roadmap. As a firm expands in size across the Service Organizational Strata, the production planning activity becomes more important to ensure the work is coordinated, deadlines are met, and clients are happy.

Capacity Planning
(short- to medium-term planning; reviewed quarterly; 51 percent of firms implement)

The What: Capacity planning is typically the one planning vehicle that most service organizations seek to build, and it is owned by an operations manager, the COO, or the firm owner. It drives all your short-term planning, which is why we spent all of Chapter 6 explaining how to calculate it using the Team Structure Capacity Chart (TSCC) and MELT. While production planning is more difficult to create, capacity planning requires having as much knowledge as possible around all the planning variables involved.

The How: Most of the planning variables in capacity planning have some level of flexibility. While services demand is relatively fixed, you need to predict what the demand will be (and its mix), since it is a critical input. This is where you would apply the seven revenue considerations from Chapter 5. On the supply side, you also have some flexibility (although the table depicts this as "somewhat fixed") because capacity planning is looking at the next quarter, which affords you time to hire more people, develop more efficient processes, cross-train existing employees, request adjustments in employee hours and schedules, and much more.

Note: Remember, the goal for capacity planning is to ensure that you have the right amount, and mix, of labor supply available at the right time to match the services demand requirements (amount and mix) for the given period. As a result, when the two sides of the equation don't match, capacity planning will let you know whether you are under- or overcapacity in general terms and what specific roles you need more or less of. There is quite a bit more to capacity planning, of course, so if you're unsure, go back to Chapters 5 and 6 to review those details.

It is worth noting that in our interviews and quantitative research with service organization firm owners that many firm owners (50 percent) typically "buffer" their capacity plan by adding additional labor supply or lowering their resource availability. On average, firm owners buffer, or discount, by 11 percent. In small firms, they might either target that their services demand requirements only absorb 80 to 90 percent of their total labor supply capacity or "hire ahead" and add an additional person to the team to have spare capacity in place in case a new client comes in or there is an issue with one of the team members. Of course, all of these decisions come with the cost to carry the salaries of team members, but you can also flex through outsourcing or contractors. Larger firms might adjust the overall labor supply by reducing the "% of Time Devoted to Revenue" column on the Capacity Analysis Chart by 5 to 10 percent, or they might overestimate the total services demand to inflate the labor supply requirements.

Each of these techniques is a shortcut for dealing with the uncertainty of time. While they are effective, they aren't an exact science. The cost paid for using these techniques is in the form of lost profitability. However, according to most firm owners we interviewed, this is viewed as a better solution than having the opposite problem—not enough labor supply to meet the services demand—which leads to missed deadlines, reduced client satisfaction, and a bad reputation. These can result in long-term hits to your brand due to consistently providing, and ultimately becoming known for, poor service. As almost every firm owner has said, "I would rather have just a bit too much extra capacity on hand rather than too little."

ONCE WE PASS the time horizon of capacity planning, we move from the world of tactical planning to strategic planning. As a result, we metaphorically move from playing darts (hitting a bullseye) to playing bocce ball (getting closest to the boccia). We're no longer striving to be accurate, but rather trying to be "close enough." The first of these strategic planning methods is workforce planning.

Workforce Planning
(medium-term planning; reviewed semi-annually;
40 percent of firms implement)

The What: Workforce planning is designed to align your staffing levels with your predicted services demand. The overall goal is to understand the estimated headcount needs of the firm six months (and later) from now. As capacity planning components are leveraged when building the workforce plan, it is typically owned by the operations manager or by a strategic member of the leadership team.

The How: For most service organizations, services demand is still relatively known when looking out six months, with a minority of the demand (e.g., 20 percent) unsigned and unaccounted for. While some demand is unknown, leaders of the firm can typically predict the services demand and mix to complete this activity. Don't overcomplicate things—determine your services demand (maybe create a few different "what-if" scenarios) and then match that with the total headcount required, without spending the time and effort on completing more complex activities, like our MELT calculations.

Note: Typically firms will leverage information from the existing TSCC so they know roughly how many people in each role will be needed on staff to meet the various services demand scenarios. If you want to be more thorough, you could easily build a future-period TSCC as well, which I wouldn't suggest if you were to model the future more than six months out. Remember, this planning method is more about playing horseshoes than archery when calculating, so don't overwork it.

Annual Planning

(medium- to long-term planning; reviewed annually; 71 percent of firms implement)

The What: Owned by the leadership team, annual planning is where everything in the firm comes together to establish long-term organizational goals and strategies while breaking them down into quarterly priorities the team can build initiatives around. In the best-run organizations I have worked in, the annual plan brings line of sight from the work each person will pursue tomorrow to the strategic goals and measures the entire firm is setting out to accomplish for the upcoming year. The annual plan should also include line of sight to the firm's overall "why," vision, mission, and values, discussed in Chapter 1.

The How: A general framework we recommend leveraging for your annual plan is the OGSM framework, which stands simply for objectives, goals, strategies, and measures. It is a practical tool for linking your business strategy with firm goals, objectives, strategies, and KPIs across a one-year time horizon. Furthermore, I recommend expanding OGSM to VOGSMT by incorporating your long-term perspective (vision) with your near-term foci (tactics). This framework brings together the following six components:

- Vision: Where we are headed as an organization

- Objective: What the plan needs to achieve (overall aspiration)

- Goals: The underlying measures of success to reach the objective

- Strategies: The top three strategic priorities for the plan (big choices)

- Measures: The measures that will prove we completed our strategies

- Tactics: The specific projects (up to three each) to support the strategies

In basic terms, the VOGSMT framework ensures you have accountability and line of site to reach the new heights you desire for the upcoming year. To get started on this:

1 List out your "why," vision, mission, and values.

2 Understand where you will be at the end of this current calendar year (baseline) and set the goals for the upcoming fiscal year. Those become your objectives (written in words), and they are supported by your goals (written as the numerical measures of those objectives).

3 Break down your annual objectives and goals into the strategic levers that will drive that outcome. That is embodied by the strategies (written in words) and measures (accountability; written as the numerical measures of those strategies).

4 Empower your team to take ownership and design the tactics they'll deploy to deliver on the strategies and measures that ladder up to deliver on the objectives and goals.

Note: The VOGSMT framework enables your leadership team to define the objectives for the year and then break them down into the strategies that are needed to be successful. In addition, it empowers the team to determine the initiatives that need to occur quarter over quarter to meet the strategic goals, while giving them the weight of accountability to ensure those goals are met. Like we said at the beginning of this section, the VOGSMT ensures line of sight to accomplish the overarching goal of the firm over a one-year time horizon.

Example:

- Vision: "We help small business restaurant owners reach their dreams through brand advice, local visibility, and technology."

- Objective: To become the leading creative agency with restauranters in our region.

- Goals: To increase our branding projects by 25 percent over the next year (to surpass the sales revenue of our nearest competitor).

- Strategies: Drive referrals from our prior branding clients and upcoming speaking engagements and podcast appearances.

- Measures: Get five referrals per quarter that result in at least one new branding client per quarter.

- Tactics: Conduct one outbound call per day to an existing (or prior) client, incentivizing referrals in exchange for free digital marketing advice.

Horizon Planning
(long-term planning; reviewed annually; 42 percent of firms implement)

The What: The purpose of horizon planning is to ensure your service organization can navigate and transform as the market and world around it changes over time. Since horizon planning spans from tomorrow through five years and beyond, it contains the most uncertainty of all the planning methods. It is managed by the firm owners and built leveraging input from senior leadership. The goal is to understand how to balance your activities in the near term (defined by the annual plan) with emerging innovations coming into fruition in the medium term (e.g., the next one to two years), with resources added to place some bets to enable transformation in the long term (e.g., the next three to five years). Horizon planning is broken into three discrete horizon buckets:

- [Horizon 1] Immediate needs: Extend and defend core business

- [Horizon 2] Emerging opportunities: Build emerging businesses or service lines

- [Horizon 3] Future transformation: Create viable options and deliver new innovations

Note: Horizon planning is a calculated approach to strategic planning to ensure the right investments are made in time to keep the firm ahead of the curve, while ensuring the resources are available to meet the needs of the annual plan. As most service organizations that are the focus of this book don't have the bandwidth to conduct horizon planning, we won't go into greater depth on it specifically, but as you become more sophisticated with your planning over time, it is the next step beyond annual planning to ensure the long-term success of your firm.

Planning: Variables, Attributes, and Methods

Using the following Time Horizon Planning Matrix tables, let's explore how planning variables and attributes necessitate and define our seven planning methods. In both tables, our planning methods will be listed on the side, ordered from those existing in the near team (e.g., work prioritization) to those in the long term (e.g., horizon planning). The first table will outline the planning *variables*, while the second table will specify the planning *attributes*.

In the Time Horizon Planning Matrix: Planning Variables table, you'll see there are four variables that influence how we plan over time:

- Resource availability
- Production capability
- Labor supply
- Services demand

Resource availability is the combination of both employee capacity and working schedule. More specifically, employee capacity is the time an individual employee contractually agrees to give you as their employer, in a given time period (e.g., 40 hours/week), and their working schedule is the timeframe within each time period that they have agreed to work (e.g., 9 am to 5 pm, Monday through

Friday). An employee's capacity ranges between fixed (near-term) and variable (long-term), as time worked leads to wages earned and the employee's ability to plan for a money shortfall or windfall. An employee's working schedule ranges between inflexible (near-term) and flexible (long-term), since family and near-term commitments make it hard to adjust a work schedule on short notice, but further out on the calendar there's more time and space to be flexible.

Time Horizon Planning Matrix: Planning Variables

Planning Methods	Resource Availability	Production Capability	Labor Supply	Services Demand
Work Prioritization	Inflexible	Rigid	Fixed	Known
Load Balancing				
Production Planning				
Capacity Planning				
Workforce Planning				
Annual Planning				
Horizon Planning	Flexible	Influenceable	Solvable	Unknown

Production capability is your production team's ability to produce work efficiently (e.g., MELT) and flexibly (e.g., TSCC) to meet the revenue planned over a given period. This is the intersection of your resources and recipes. When focusing on the resources, it relates to the skills they bring to the job, their flexibility to do a variety of work, and the level of their productivity as defined by MELT. When related to the recipes, it is the efficiency of the system of processes, the technology used to amplify their skills, and the operations management techniques in place. When measuring production capability, we look at the flexibility (e.g., skills, measured from inflexible to flexible) of the organization to meet the revenue demand plus the efficiency (measured from rigid to influenceable) by which the work can be delivered. Many factors can influence flexibility (e.g., higher skilled labor, cross-training, flexible staffing) and efficiency (e.g., operations management, continuous process improvement, streamlined operations).

Labor supply is the availability of the right resources (e.g., labor) to match the expected revenue. In the near term, this will represent your present team and their related production ability. As you move further out into the future, this will represent where and how you will find new labor when necessary (e.g., junior staff versus seasoned technicians) and how quickly you can hire, train, and deploy new team members into production. When measuring labor supply, it is defined by whether the resources are fixed (unable to change or add) and solvable (supply and time exist to source and train).

Services demand is the market's request for your organization's services. Remember our discussion in Chapter 5 on planning future revenue and the seven revenue considerations? The concepts in Chapter 5 are directly relevant to this variable. In the near term, services demand will represent your present client list and their service needs, whether recurring and predictable or project-based and unpredictable. As you move further out into the long term, this will represent the strength of your lead gen/marketing efforts, the probability you will successfully close those leads, and the effectiveness and timeliness of onboarding a new client, among other things. We measure services demand from known (demand is fixed) to unknown (demand is uncertain).

From the table, we can determine how these planning variables change in response to time. As time gets greater (long term), labor supply and services demand become more abstract and unpredictable, while resource availability and production capability become more flexible. As time gets closer to today (near term), labor supply and services demand become fixed (i.e., known), while resource availability and production capability become more rigid (i.e., inflexible). It is this constraint of the planning variables in the near term and the open-endedness of them in the long term that require us to use differing planning methods (e.g., work prioritization, load balancing, etc.).

For instance, in the long term, I need to know what overall revenue I expect so I have enough time to hire sufficient resources to ensure it can be completed. In the near term, I know the client deliverable deadlines that are approaching, and I need to know who is doing what work at what time so I don't miss a deadline. Different time horizons mean we need to plan at different altitudes.

Now let's look at the second Time Horizon Planning Matrix table. Where the previous table focused on planning variables, this table focuses on planning attributes. See the table called the Time Horizon Planning Matrix: Planning Attributes. Down the left-hand side, the chart is again broken into various planning methods. We will again use these as time spans from near term (today) to the long term (future). Beside each planning method, we have provided the attributes to further define when they are relevant, how often they are reviewed, who owns the planning, and what it oversees.

Time Horizon Planning Matrix: Planning Attributes

Planning Methods	Time Period	Review Frequency	Ownership	Focus
Work Prioritization	Next week	Daily	Individual contributor	My work
Load Balancing	Next month	Weekly	Team lead(s)	Individual team
Production Planning	This quarter	Monthly	Team manager(s)	Between teams
Capacity Planning	Next quarter	Quarterly	Operations manager	Across teams
Workforce Planning	Next 6 months	Semi-annually	Leadership team	All resources
Annual Planning	Next year	Annually	Executive team	3 Rs
Horizon Planning	Next 5 years	Annually	Partners/ owners	Organizational growth

When looking at the planning attributes, the ownership of the various planning methods directly relates to what we discussed in Chapter 3 (Service Organizational Strata) and Chapter 4 (span of control, division of labor, and pod/departmentalization). It also depends on how your organization has determined the scaffolding that might be represented in your Team Structure Capacity Chart from Chapter 6. If you manage a small firm, the ownership beyond work prioritization (which is owned by each individual contributor) might just be you, the owner. If you're managing a large firm, the ownership might represent the collective set of all roles, which is a combination of team leaders, operations manager, leadership, and yourself. As well, some firms have designed their operations around their clients, so their team leaders might be called "client service managers," while others have designed them around their services, so their team leaders might be called "project managers." Don't worry about the title or role of the owner for each planning method, but rather the altitude at which that person operates. You will see that the ownership will move from a low altitude (individual contributor) in work prioritization to a high altitude (you!) in annual and horizon planning.

How to Actually Do Planning over Time

With our planning methods defined, how do these tools work together in aggregate? Let's start out in the future, where things are most uncertain, and walk back the timeline to where we are today. We'll use a fictitious accountancy named Balanced Books (which generates $2 million in revenue per year) to guide our journey.

If we talk about long-term planning, your planning variables are generally flexible and uncertain. During this time horizon, you really don't know what anything will be: (a) services demand may be growing or contracting (not typically staying the same); (b) labor supply could be what you have today, but it will probably shift; and (c) both who you have (resource availability) and how efficient they are (production capability) likely will be at least a little different in a year. So with all four planning variables uncertain, you need to try to constrain one variable to help determine the other three. Note that constraining one of the variables is an obvious example of how you design your services organization. Many owners feel like they have no power, but this complex chapter is displaying the power we all have in our design, as complex as it may be.

The variable that you can seek to constrain as a first priority is services demand—your revenue. When you determine your services demand, you can complete all the other planning methods. So let's get going.

1. Demand forecast. How do you set your services demand for the year? You perform what-if scenarios to estimate it based on your best guess of what you can expect in the upcoming year. Through creating differing what-if scenarios, you can ladder into the scenario that seems most likely based on what you know today (this goes back to the seven revenue considerations in Chapter 5: volume, timing, complexity, cadence, novelty, placement, and probability).

Your job as a firm owner is to determine this critical component of the plan (which is a subset of your annual plan). When doing this, reflect on the capacity complexities we discussed in Chapter 7. Once you set the overall annual services demand, then you need to model it over time to break it down quarter over quarter. With that, congratulations! You now have your demand forecast (which is annually set and updated quarterly), and your first piece of the planning puzzle is complete.

When thinking of our company, Balanced Books, we might do the following activities to create our demand forecast:

- Review our current engagements (client a, client b, etc.) and model out the ones that will renew next year (75 percent will renew; equivalent to $1.5 million in revenue).

- Review our services mix (e.g., client accounting, CFO advisory, and tax services) and adjust it per our expectations and goals (e.g., 40, 20, and 30 percent, respectively).

- Set the year-over-year (YoY) revenue growth target (e.g., 20 percent YoY) based on current promised engagements and expected new revenue (need to generate $2.4 million in revenue next year).

- Build out the demand forecast based on mix, amounts, and timing of the revenue.
  - Client accounting = $960,000 (recurring monthly)
  - CFO advisory = $480,000 (recurring quarterly)
  - Tax services = $720,000 (recurring annually)

2. Workforce plan. You will typically complete your workforce plan semi-annually, because revenue is defined (demand), costs are set (resources), and profitability can be determined. The workforce plan involves determining what resources in what roles are needed to match the demand forecasted for each quarterly time period. For Balanced Books, it would outline how many bookkeepers, accountants, admins, CFO advisory, management, et cetera, are needed to be able to at least meet the services demand projected. For instance, we calculated that a single bookkeeper can manage $120,000 of client accounting revenue and we need an admin for every 100 clients. This corresponds to 8 bookkeepers and 2 admins (as each bookkeeper typically manages 25 clients). This sets your resource mix and quantity for each role, assuming some pre-set role-based productivity measure. While this fixes the supply problem of the equation, it doesn't really define the production capability, because you don't have all the resources, nor do you really know their MELT. You just have an approximation for this, and you will need a buffer (based on your risk tolerance level) to ensure you can successfully meet the demand forecast you have set. So for now, production capability is semi-fixed.

3. Capacity plan. The next step is to fully define the production-capability part of the equation. You will typically do this every quarter for the upcoming quarter. At this point, the supply and demand sides of the equation are fixed, and you've shrunken the planning period to something manageable (a quarter) but far enough out that the other planning variables are still flexible enough to work with. You know

- what work has to be done;
- what people you have (or should have hired);
- how efficient those people are and what skills they have; and
- roughly what their work schedules will be.

Now you can complete your capacity planning using MELT discounting. This will make clear if you truly have the right resources at the right time to complete the work promised. However, it does not optimize for profitability. It just defines if you can or can't meet the demand forecasted. In our example, we would take the information we have (demand, workforce plan, and roles) and work through the same exercise we did in Chapter 6 by creating our TSCC, determining MELT for our team members, and completing our Capacity Analysis Chart.

4. Production plan. This is typically created quarterly but updated monthly. A production plan determines which resources will be assigned to complete certain projects at a given time to optimize for a given variable (or set of variables). Do you want to minimize missed deadlines with clients? Do you want to maximize profitability by using the lowest-skilled or lowest-paid labor for each type of task you have? All of this is constrained by the people you have, the capacity they have to give, the productivity by which they will operate, and the set of skills and roles they can perform.

To construct a production plan properly requires a lot of data, effort, and understanding of the firm. It also takes a bit of time to complete. For our example, we would lay out the remaining current and upcoming quarters, by project, and allocate who works on which projects. For client accounting, we typically complete the bookkeeping by the fifth of the month, accounting and reconciliations by the twentieth of the month, and CFO advisory (if added on) by the twenty-fifth of the month. Since we have two hundred clients served by eight bookkeepers (and two admins), we would allocate the bookkeepers (or retain their existing allocations) for the twenty-five clients that they would be working on for each given month.

Now, let's move within the quarter to a time horizon like this month. At this point in time, everything is fixed and inflexible. You have the deadlines you promised (and the work involved), you have the resources and their defined production capability, and you should have an idea of who does what work. We should be good, right? Wrong. There are and always will be shocks to the system.

Here are a few examples. A new, large, important prospective client gives the firm a call (demand goes up). A staff member must go on leave (resources decrease). Another staff member gets sick (resource availability shifts). Unexpectedly, one of the fixed variables changes values, throwing all our good efforts of planning out the window.

With your production plan now a bit sideways, you are trying to determine a new optimal production plan. This is typically accomplished by foregoing profitability and optimizing for deadline completion (even at the expense of work quality). But, at this point, the firm is unfortunately out of one key component—time. It's time for...

5. Load balancing. This is the art of moving work between people so that it's balanced between the various remaining members on the team. It may also bring into the equation non-billable resources and their resource time to fill in the gaps. For some large firms, this "stealing" from non-billable resources or overtime is destructive, and they would rather over-hire to prevent it (though this can be costly for smaller firms). Other firms either are unaware or accept that it can happen and will overstretch capacity (overwork team members or do the work themselves as owners) or deprioritize low-value work to maximize profitability. In our example, one of our bookkeepers goes on leave for a given month. We would then reallocate those 25 accounting clients from that team member and assign them to a utility player (perhaps an accountant with spare capacity), distribute them across the bookkeeper pool (forcing overtime), or assign them to a senior manager (stealing non-billable management time to billable client work time).

6. Work prioritization. The last time period to deal with is *this week*. Unlike the other planning activities that might be at a leadership level (demand forecasting, annual planning, workforce planning, and capacity planning) or manager level (production planning, load balancing), at this point the planning is at an individual level.

From all the other planning activities, I, as an individual contributor, know what work needs to be done. However, I need to decide in what order I do the work based on the optimization criteria set by my management. Is completing the maximum amount of work assigned based on count the most important? Is completing the maximum amount of work based on value the most important? What level of quality is required? Does this vary based on the client or client type? Am I defaulting to doing the easiest work first? These are the questions the individual contributor has to ask and answer to create their work prioritization—to know what work to do in what order for today, tomorrow, this week, and maybe even next week.

The work prioritization plan is the final piece of the planning puzzle. In our example, I (your author Ian) am one of the bookkeepers on the team. On Monday, I review all the work that needs to be completed by Friday and rank order the jobs to be done by the revenue value of each client. I then work through my job list throughout the week, monitoring my progress day by day to ensure I can make all the deadlines. If I can't make the deadlines, I alert my manager so they can reassign low-revenue-value clients to someone else in the interim.

While we use operations management to combat variability, we use planning to combat uncertainty. As time expands into the future, it makes the four planning variables more uncertain. To handle the uncertainty, we need to constrain our variables, like Gary did, so we can use our planning methods at different points in time. We start by fixing our services demand in our annual plan, our labor supply in our workforce plan, our production capability in our capacity plan, and then our resource availability in our production plan. In the short and near term, we are making difficult choices through load balancing and work prioritization to maximize our work delivery at the expense of internal metrics like profitability, quality control, and employee satisfaction. By following this planning methodology, you can accomplish what Gary accomplished in his firm—more predictability, more clarity, and fewer sleepless nights.

I realize that this chapter is a lot to take in and expect you might read it more than once to have the puzzle pieces come together. As we mentioned at the beginning of the book, leading a service organization is complicated. As a result, you need to be intentional about setting your business strategy and then breaking it down from a long-term goal to a short-term tactical plan. The effort you spend working through these planning methods will enable you to absorb the inevitable shocks to your human-based system and give you confidence to accelerate through the scaling plateau speed wobble that you'll undoubtably face (and conquer). But don't fear, because you aren't alone. We understand that this is complicated, and we are also here to help. Jason and I have included additional resources, tools, and training on the book's website.

12

Building Something Truly Valuable

Ian Vacin

When I was twenty-seven, I went to graduate school in India and took a trip to Nepal to hike much of the 118-mile Annapurna Circuit over a ten-day period. At that time, the trek was a bit more rugged than it is now. There weren't any roads—just hiking trails. The trail starts at 2,493 feet, goes up or down each day about 3,000 feet, and reaches its highest point of 17,769 feet. The Annapurna Circuit is not as famous as going to Mount Everest base camp, but it is a beautiful journey along the top of the world.

Each day I hiked, I eyeballed the next high point in the far distance and set a goal to conquer it. In my quest, I was able to conquer some fantastic highs like Poon Hill (10,532 feet), Muktinath (12,172 feet), and finally Thorong La Pass (17,769 feet). But I also experienced the lows of hiking downhill (not my favorite) and walking through the long Kali Gandaki riverbed (one of the deepest gorges in the world) in a massive sandstorm. All the while, I would get glances at the highest peak in the Annapurna Massif, Annapurna I (26,545 feet).

249

My journey through Nepal is similar to the journey we take as entrepreneurs. At times, we reach new highs. At other times, we reach new lows. And sometimes, we hit a plateau that just doesn't seem to end. It is that journey that defines who we are and what our organizations become. Over the course of this book, we discussed what it takes and what you need to do to grow your service organization, manage and plan its resources, and conquer the scaling plateaus that have and will exist in your future. But where does it all lead? What does success finally look like? Can we reach and conquer that highest peak? How do we measure that, what is it, and how do we maximize it?

For service organizations, we can squarely say that success is defined around the human, and we trust this book has given you a lot of the tools you need to scale successfully with your team. Mainly a lot of your success comes down to who you are as the founder, owner, and/or leader. What are you trying to achieve? That is really all that matters. After doing this for almost thirty years, I can say that the biggest peak I've had to climb is myself. I had to stop comparing myself and my firm to others, and I had to recognize my own special value that I brought to the world of entrepreneurship. As service entrepreneurs, we have to come to the place where we realize that there isn't a destination we'll finally arrive at where we will stop caring or working or thinking about our businesses. We have to come to the place where we learn to enjoy the journey... with the highest peaks and the lowest valleys. Now may be a time to recommit yourself to what it truly means to be a leader of a growing service firm. Which means aiming to maximize your enterprise value.

Defining Enterprise Value

Over the course of the book, we have mentioned repeatedly that size of revenue, number of employees, and number of clients shouldn't be the goal. Those numbers are thrown around by your peers at conferences and events and used for posturing like a peacock train-rattling for a mate. When I watch the show *Shark Tank* with my kids and they mention how successful this firm owner has become when they sold $X million of goods, I immediately retort, "But they haven't told you the other side of the equation. What was their cost of goods sold, and what percentage of the company do they still even own? What did they sacrifice or give up to get that?" Perhaps I am always skeptical, but the truth of success lies in the numbers that really matter: your ability to produce profit from your efforts. That is, the ability to create real value in the world where it didn't exist before and to do that repeatedly over time.

When measuring and comparing firms on purely analytical terms, enterprise value (EV) is a common mechanism. While EV is defined as including market capitalization, total debt, and cash and cash equivalents, most people think of EV as just market capitalization. For the purposes of simplicity, let's assume EV equals market capitalization.

Market capitalization doesn't care per se about the number of clients or employees. The more profitable a company is seen to be, the higher its market capitalization is likely to be, as buyers are willing to pay more to acquire the business. Calculating market capitalization can be done through several methods:

Asset-based approach: Calculate the value of your assets and then subtract total liabilities from total assets to determine a net asset value. This isn't as feasible for service organizations because they are thin on hard assets, like manufacturing equipment, and over-indexed on off-balance sheet assets, like human capital, relationships, recurring revenue, intellectual property, and brand reputation.

Comparable company analysis: Like buying a house, this method uses comparables of publicly available info to derive industry multiples like EV/EBITDA or EV/revenue. Then, you apply the multiple to your firm's numbers. While it's possible for large, public businesses, this isn't an option for small, private businesses unless you are using a broker. As a result, this is another method we can't typically leverage.

Discounted cash flows: Project the company's future free cash flows (cash left over after covering all capital and operating expenses) and discount them back to present value using a discount rate. If you can't remember your Finance 101, discounting a single, future cash flow would be: present value = cash flow $/ (1+r)^t$ where r = discount rate per time period and t = quantity of time periods. This is a viable option, but it requires a service organization to have very predictable earnings (and a calculator!). This method is often used when valuing small service businesses that are under $1 million in revenue.

Revenue (or EBITDA) multiple: To calculate, simply apply an industry-driven multiplier to a firm's revenue (or EBITDA) to estimate its value. A revenue multiple is preferred for valuing small firms (under $1 million in revenue) and an EBITDA multiple for larger firms (although EBITDA is becoming more popular for all sizes of firms). For most transactions with private, service organizations, the revenue is calculated using the trailing twelve months of actual revenue (versus current fiscal year forecasted revenue). The multiplier will range in value from laggards (low-performing firms) to leaders (high-performing firms). For service organization buyers and sellers, the revenue multiple method is the most often used within the knowledge work industries (e.g., accounting, legal).

In our quantitative research for the book, 60 percent of respondents preferred the revenue multiple method (with 68 percent using the trailing twelve months of actual revenue) and provided these average revenue multiples for the accounting profession:

- Laggard (bottom quartile): 1.0 times revenue
- Transitioning (second quartile): 1.2 times revenue
- Expanding (third quartile): 1.5 times revenue
- Leader (top quartile): 2.0 times revenue

Note that each service industry will have different revenue multiples and those revenue multiple tiers will change in value over time. The multiples provided here are anecdotal only.

For an individual firm's multiple, remember that it isn't just about the revenue itself, but the *quality* of the revenue and whether the engine of growth is sustainable. Buyers typically view a possible purchase from a pessimistic point of view, anchor using a laggard category multiple, and look for factors to increase the revenue multiple based on the performance of the firm. Sellers view the equation from the opposite perspective and look at factors that require them to decrease the revenue multiple from a leader category multiple. Factors that will devalue the revenue multiple include

- high customer concentration;

- low gross margins;

- slow (or slowing) revenue growth;

- non-recurring (or lumpy) revenue;

- weak competitive advantage (e.g., lack of niche focus);

- high churn and attrition rates;

- increasing regulatory risk embedded in the client base;

- poor unit economics (e.g., customer acquisition cost is higher than customer lifetime value);

- weak leadership team (or financial controls); and

- lack of operational scale (or inability to scale).

Let's look at an example using revenue multiples to calculate enterprise value in simple terms. Over the past twelve months, your accounting firm generated $2 million in revenue, has 16 employees, and has 100 business clients. Over the past few years, you have continually grown revenue more than 30 percent year over year (like Mike Libbey from YBL), your average gross margins are at 50 percent (following the advice of Dan Gertrudes from Growth-Lab), you have invested in process improvement and technology (like Mark Shipton from Ignite CPA), you have a successful niche service line (like Jason Blumer advises), and you have rebuilt your leadership team and structure using Gino Wickman's EOS (like Jessica Hennessey and Mary Inman from 3 Media Web). In this situation, your business would be subjectively considered as either a top-performing expanding business (third quartile) or an overall leader (top quartile). As such, you would choose a revenue multiplier of around two times the trailing twelve months' actual revenue, and your enterprise value would then be calculated as EV = market capitalization = $2 million × 2 = $4 million.

While revenue is a variable in the enterprise value equation, the revenue multiplier is the key factor in driving enterprise value. The revenue multiplier incorporates all the efforts that you and your team put into the business day after day and year after year to make it a better business. It is interesting to note that if you want to sell your firm and work to increase your enterprise value prior to selling, the efforts needed to increase value are the same efforts needed to create a better business overall (which are the concepts taught in this book). In many cases, firm owners pursue the journey to sell, just to realize that, after having transformed their unperforming business into a well-performing one, they no longer want to sell.

Chasing the Global Maximum

Let's revisit the story about Chad Davis and Josh Zweig (LiveCA) that we discussed in Chapter 6, because there is more to the story and it shines a spotlight on why and how to obtain the global maximum of enterprise value.

GLOBAL MAXIMUM

The absolute largest value of a function, even when multiple local maximums may exist. For instance, a business might have a set of characteristics that drives a local enterprise value maximum for when they are fewer than 8 employees, another between 8 and 20 employees, and another over 20 employees, but across all sizes only one global, absolute enterprise value can exist.

I have known Chad Davis for over a decade. He's someone that I call a colleague, mentor, visionary, and friend. Over the years, we have spent time discussing what it takes to grow and scale service organizations and geeking out on subjects like capacity planning. For years, I would ask how his business was doing, how many staff he had grown to, and how many clients they served. And for years, he would plow through scaling plateau after scaling plateau until he reached over 120 employees and almost 500 business clients in 2023. Like me, he had climbed to the top of another insurmountable peak. But, when we chatted in early 2024, the conversation was very different, and LiveCA was now almost half the size. I was shocked. Had he hit the sandstorm that I hit when I was hiking in Nepal? What happened?

It was during those trips chasing sunsets in the RV with his family (and significant financial stresses) that Chad (as well as Josh) made time to think and reflect about the business. Working closely with their leadership team to turn things around, it was clear they didn't want to push through the next scaling plateau. What they learned from reflection and looking deep into the merits of the company was that it had a very strong leadership team, incredible managers, and a team that loved what they did and who they did it for. So that meant dropping services (CFO/automation consulting) and doubling down on things they did well (controllership, bookkeeping, payroll, AP, and tax), all while moving away from value pricing. It was never a consideration to grow to 150, 200, or even 250 employees. The stress wasn't worth it.

There's something special about leaning into your core values, slowing down, and providing a stable, calm environment for your team, who might typically be used to the chaos of client work. Chad's epiphany was that the answer lies in finding the global maximum of profitability—LiveCA's very own enterprise value.

As I mentioned earlier in the book, my background is rooted in industrial engineering and operations research. To put that in simple terms, I love math, I like solving problems, and I can't stand it when something is inefficient. In mathematics, derivatives are all about finding the maximums and minimums of a function. If you take the first derivative of a function and set it equal to zero, you find the critical points that exist at a local extremum. Do a first derivative test by exploring the sign of the derivative on either side of the critical point, and you learn whether it is a local maximum or local minimum. If you find all the critical points—all local extrema—and look at the highest and lowest values, then you have found the global maximum and minimum, respectively. Visually, the function looks like the Minimums and Maximums diagram.

Minimums and Maximums

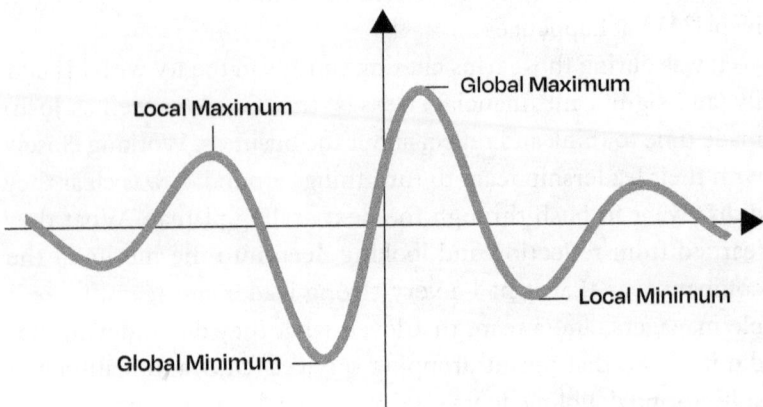

It is like my hike in Nepal. When you look across the mountain-scape, you see many peaks in the distance. Each is a local maximum. But there is always one peak, in this case Annapurna I, that is highest—our global maximum. Scan further to your left or right, and the peaks get smaller in the distance, and your mountainscape turns into a landscape. The mountainscape example here is akin to your business growth journey representing all the highs (local maximums) and lows (local minimums) that you'll undoubtably face. Our highest peak doesn't appear as we look farther and farther to the right, but, rather, it's somewhere in the middle. This is similar to our businesses, where the global maximum isn't at the point where your firm is the largest in revenue or headcount, but somewhere in the middle where everything lines up for what *you want* from your business. As you make your way through your own journey of growth, note that you'll hit a lot of highs and lows that you can see (the Local depictions on the chart), but you may not know that the hardest, and greatest, parts of your journey are just around the corner (the Global depictions on the chart).

Yuck, math, I know, but it is an important concept for our service organizations and our goal as entrepreneurial firm owners seeking our own enterprise value. Does an Olympian compete to get second place? Do you feel satisfied that you hiked the second-highest mountain when the highest one was within your grasp? We are human. We want to reach the top (the maximum), and we want that for our businesses as well.

Back to Chad and LiveCA and their decision to shrink their firm by half. Why would they do that? As they grew from 2 to 20, to 60, and then to 120, the firm they knew and loved changed—and not for the better. LiveCA is very driven by the organization's vision, mission, and values. One of the things they say on their website is, "We believe that freedom in your job brings more meaning to your life." With the increased firm size, the scaffolding required was in conflict with the central vision of the firm itself and causing friction for the staff, their clients, and Chad and Josh. They were chasing revenue and firm size rather than overall profitability. The mathematical function of success wasn't adding up like it should. "The lesson learned," Chad said, "was the larger the company grew, the more management was required (and the less profitable it became)."

At that point, Chad and Josh began the journey to seek not a local maximum but rather a global maximum, as they knew they were going to have to downsize the firm. So they built and analyzed various business models at different firm sizes, exploring what it might mean to be at 40, 60, or 80 employees. In some aspects, it was a leveraged pyramid, since they knew exactly what service lines they wanted to continue to offer, how many people one person could manage, what the theoretical capacity was for a given production pod, and what the firm scaffolding would need to be to support that size and structure. When they looked at 80 employees, there was too much costly management. At 40 people, there just weren't enough levels of support or management in order for people to experience different things (like new roles, new work, and time off), and the stress on people would be too high. That was unacceptable. But at 60 people, Chad and Josh found something very interesting. In Chad's words:

> When we modeled the business at 60 people, we were
>
> - five to six times more profitable than at 120 people;
> - only one to two times less profitable than at 40 people; and
> - four times more profitable than at 80 people.

Sixty was their magic number for their global maximum enterprise value. It optimized the usage of their pods. It minimized the amount of firm scaffolding required. It delivered on the values and culture they had spent years cultivating. The mathematical function's first derivative was zero, and it all added up!

After even further evaluation, Chad and Josh's analysis showed that they should never get bigger than 64 people to optimize both profit and culture. So in 2024, they made the change and downsized the firm from 120 to 60 staff and reduced their clients served by almost 40 percent. Painful? Extremely. Necessary? Definitely.

Successful? Without a doubt. But remember, enterprise value for Chad and Josh wasn't just about maximizing profitability. Enterprise value is a balance of the various components of what you value in a business. And, as we mentioned at the beginning of the book, this is both what it means and what it takes to be a service-based entrepreneurial firm owner.

Throughout the journey of this book, our goal has been to bring you to here—a place of wisdom where you have learned enough to become a new type of entrepreneur. An entrepreneur who will be intentional in the pursuit of their goals. An entrepreneur who knows what they want and has the tools, knowledge, and blueprint to scale with purpose. It is when you put all the pieces we've discussed thus far together that you too can find, pursue, and achieve your unique global maximum.

Driving Your Enterprise Value

Jason Blumer

Now it's your turn to learn what your global maximum is. It's okay if you don't know what it is now, but Ian and I wrote this book to give you the tools to climb the mountain and figure it out as you go. As we said before, don't compare where you are to anyone else, because no one has this figured out. It's a journey, not a destination.

But the book has also been making one key overarching point: Service organizations don't build themselves. Everyone can build something great, but *you* will drive it if it's going to happen. You must take risks and you must make moves. Balanced with that is the fact that you will fail. You might think that failure is proof that you just don't know how to hire, or maybe you weren't made for this, or you probably should just go get a job. These are all false. When that team member leaves without you expecting it, that is a hard defeat. But what do you do then? You have to figure it out, so you do. And that is you driving toward your own enterprise value. You start learning because you have no choice.

Josh Huggins went through this journey of building the enterprise value of Chattanooga, Tennessee–based Whiteboard. The agency was started by Eric Brown and Taylor Jones, and both founders saw the need to bring in Josh as the president to help take the business where it really needed to go. Josh is a reformed entrepreneur himself, having started and sold many of his own small business endeavors. However, Josh left entrepreneurship behind to serve two great founders, rather than be one himself. When he decided to join Eric and Taylor, they became the perfect mullet: Eric and Taylor are the entrepreneurs (the party in the back), while Josh is the business in the front. In building Whiteboard, Eric and Taylor had the foresight to realize that they could not properly scale the company the way they wanted to. So they found someone with the learned skill that could do it with them. Some of the stories in this book have been about the need for service entrepreneurs to shrink their companies as they learned "what it means." Whiteboard did what it had to do to scale larger, with purpose. And they have succeeded.

Few entrepreneurs have the foresight that Eric and Taylor had. Many founders keep pushing down the road of building the way an entrepreneur builds. But entrepreneurs are gunslingers, and a business scaling with purpose must eventually have a sheriff in town. Sometimes the entrepreneur can do both (we talked about this in Chapter 4, where we asked if you are a leader, an entrepreneur, or an entrepreneurial leader). Sometimes an entrepreneurial leader can take crazy risks to create amazing enterprise value, while also bringing order to the service organization to cull the chaos over time as it grows. But not everyone can, and Eric and Taylor recognized that, so they put Josh in charge to lead the implementation of the order that would allow them to grow their original vision larger and safer with purpose.

Josh had to make some difficult changes to the business, consolidate teams, departmentalize around services, and remove some of the team members. Josh also leveraged the capacity management techniques of MELT in Chapter 6 to bring clarity and control to the capacity output of the team. He knew to intuitively add scaffolding as Whiteboard grew over time.

The result of these changes is that Whiteboard was able to grow without stalling, surmount the resulting scaling plateaus that come with growth, and become a company that provides great service, allowing the team to enjoy their work. Eric and Taylor have a rare ability to see that the business they'd founded had taken on a life of its own. This always happens to organizations as they grow: Eventually the business becomes decidedly separate from the founder and owners. What is an entrepreneur to do at this point? As we mentioned in Chapter 3, they have to do what is best for the organization and give it what it needs to grow—freedom to become itself. Josh was the gift to Whiteboard that allowed it to become a real business and drive true enterprise value.

Julie Shipp was that for me. I had founded other companies in the past that flamed out with debt in tow as I did whatever I wanted. After observing me trying to grow up for a few years, Julie said, "I'm not an entrepreneur." I disagreed and said, "Of course you are, you are my partner and the owner of our businesses." She taught me my next lesson: that an entrepreneur and an owner are not necessarily the same thing. No matter how many people try to push Julie to the forefront of our businesses (and many do), she is quite clear and content in her role as my partner and owner. She knows what she wants, and she knows that successful businesses need order, intention, and a deep care for the clients and the team. She intuitively leads that in our businesses.

Julie was what the businesses needed to scale, while I had to do a lot of growing up. And I'm glad to say that I did. I was a failed entrepreneur turned business owner turned CEO, and I now accept every day what it means to lead two growing businesses. As I say at our conferences, looking at my calendar will make your butt crack sweat. It takes a lot of work, and it may take bringing in someone else eventually. That may not be a choice you have to make, but it's one I knew I had to make. Are you the business leader that your growing organization needs? Maybe you need to grow up. Maybe you need someone else to help you lead. Maybe you need to stop getting "whatever you want." The long-term enterprise value of your organization requires that you figure this out.

Thirty years into my entrepreneurial career, I can tell you that—to use Ian's metaphors—after climbing up to Thorong La Pass and then down into the Kali Gandaki Gorge a thousand times over, you'll see the next mountain as really just another hill to walk over. The journey of entrepreneurship becomes less crushing, and you learn that this defeat won't be your demise. You do have to still do the work, but you will, and your mindset will be different now too. Because you'll know that you are simply learning (as painful as that can be). And this book will be here as a reference for you to come back to time and again to keep learning the lessons we will all be learning together.

In our Thriveal community, part of the job my partner and I do is to remind the members that "you change lives; don't forget that." I say that often when we get off a monthly community group call or end a masterclass together. Service entrepreneurs need that reminder daily. So here it is again: You change lives; don't forget that. We lead human organizations. Though that comes with an emotional weight of sacrifice for you the founder/owner, as well as the complexity of the subjects we've tackled in this book, it also comes with the joy of seeing others grow and fight their own demons, knowing that you, the service entrepreneur, are part of what changed their lives.

All of this is changing you too. Good—let it change you. Scaling a service organization will not leave you the same as when you started. Embrace this and grow to become a new person on the journey. You may be just a bit wiser now, equipped with much more data, information, and tools than you were before you started reading. And you may be overwhelmed too, wondering how you will ever apply everything we've been teaching in this book. Let's just keep going.

We've been at this a long time. We'll keep going. Will you keep going on this journey with us? We hope so. Don't give up driving the heart, soul, and profitability of your enterprise's value so that you can thrive at the right size and do it with purpose.

We're rooting for you, service entrepreneur!

Notes

Chapter 2

pg. 31   Tim Williams says... Tim Williams, "Better Is Not Different. Only Different Is Different," LinkedIn, August 19, 2020, linkedin.com/pulse/better-different-only-tim-williams.

Chapter 6

pg. 111   you are meant to place the roles... Gino Wickman, *Traction* (BenBella Books, 2011), 89.

Chapter 9

pg. 167   Stemming from the teachings of quality pioneers... Dan Ciampa, *Total Quality: A User's Guide for Implementation* (Addison Wesley Publishing, 1992), xviii; American Society for Quality, "Total Quality Management," n.d., asq.org/quality-resources/total-quality-management.

pg. 174   Lean, Lean Thinking, and Lean Manufacturing... John F. Krafcik, "Triumph of the Lean Production System," *Sloan Management Review*, 30, no. 1 (1988): 41–52, proquest.com/openview/a6938b5d5125c0061cc9881c8014c9bd; James P. Womack and Daniel T. Jones, *Lean Thinking: Banish Waste and Create Wealth in Your Corporation* (Taylor & Francis, 1996); James P. Womack, Daniel T. Jones, and Daniel Roos, *The Machine That Changed the World* (Rawson Associates Scribner, 1990).

pg. 174   As defined by the acronym DOWNTIME... Jean Cunningham, "The Eight Wastes of Lean," Lean Enterprise Institute, January 18, 2020, lean.org/the-lean-post/articles/the-eight-wastes-of-lean.

pg. 177   Lean can be combined with... David W. Dickson, "An Actuary in the World of Six Sigma," Society of Actuaries, February 2005, soa.org/library/newsletters/the-actuary-magazine/2005/february/act2005february.

pg. 182   Atul Gawande writes that checklists... Atul Gawande, *The Checklist Manifesto: How to Get Things Right* (Metropolitan Books, 2009), 120.

About the Authors

PHOTO: JUSTIN NIX

JASON M. BLUMER IS THE founder and CEO of Thriveal, a coaching, training, and educational company serving entrepreneurial CPA firm owners. He's also CEO of Blumer & Associates CPAs. He hosts the *Thrivecast* podcast and speaks regularly on reimagining professional services. Jason helps traditional accounting practices evolve into strategic advisory firms that deliver exceptional value while building scalable, profitable businesses. He lives in Greenville, South Carolina.

IAN VACIN has almost thirty years' leadership experience in technology and accounting at Karbon, Xero, and Intuit. Ian is passionate about helping accounting professionals be as successful as possible to help the small businesses they serve. He was named a Top 20 Under 40 in 2016 by the *CPA Practice Advisor* and a Marketer That Matters in 2013 by *The Wall Street Journal*. Ian has a master's in engineering management and an MBA from Northwestern University and Kellogg School of Management. He lives in Fremont, California.

WORK
WITH US

We trust this book has given you the foundation for scaling a service organization with intention. But we know this book could not address everything that is needed to scale these types of businesses. In fact, we know every service entrepreneur will (and should) take the concepts in this book and change or tweak them to suit their leadership style and their organization's approach to growth. If you need assistance with interpreting these concepts, Jason and Ian are here to help. Here are the ways we enable service organizations to scale:

Live Scaling Workshops: We hold live scaling workshops where service entrepreneurs from various industries come together for deeper teachings and demonstrations of the concepts in this book, as well as to work out their own versions of these concepts. We hope you'll consider joining us. Space is limited, so grab your seat quickly when the registration page is updated each year.

Speaking/Writing: Ian and Jason are speakers and writers at heart. We've been doing both for many years and have traveled globally teaching the concepts of growth to thousands of entrepreneurs. Many of the concepts in this book were released at conferences, spoken on stages, and shared with those we consult and coach with. If you need a speaker, additional writing, or a podcast guest, reach out to us through the contact form on our website.

Consulting/Coaching: These concepts are foundational, but they are highly context dependent, so we hope you will make them your own. However, for the service entrepreneur who needs additional help or is in a place where they cannot get unstuck, we are here to help and enter into more intimate consulting and coaching agreements with you. Just reach out.

To find out more about these opportunities, as well as updated resources shared in the book, you can reach us at scalewithpurpose.info.